AF411875

Jan Kotik

The Painterly Object

Essays by
Susan Krane and
Hans-Peter Riese

January 27 - March 18, 1984

Albright-Knox Art Gallery
Buffalo, New York

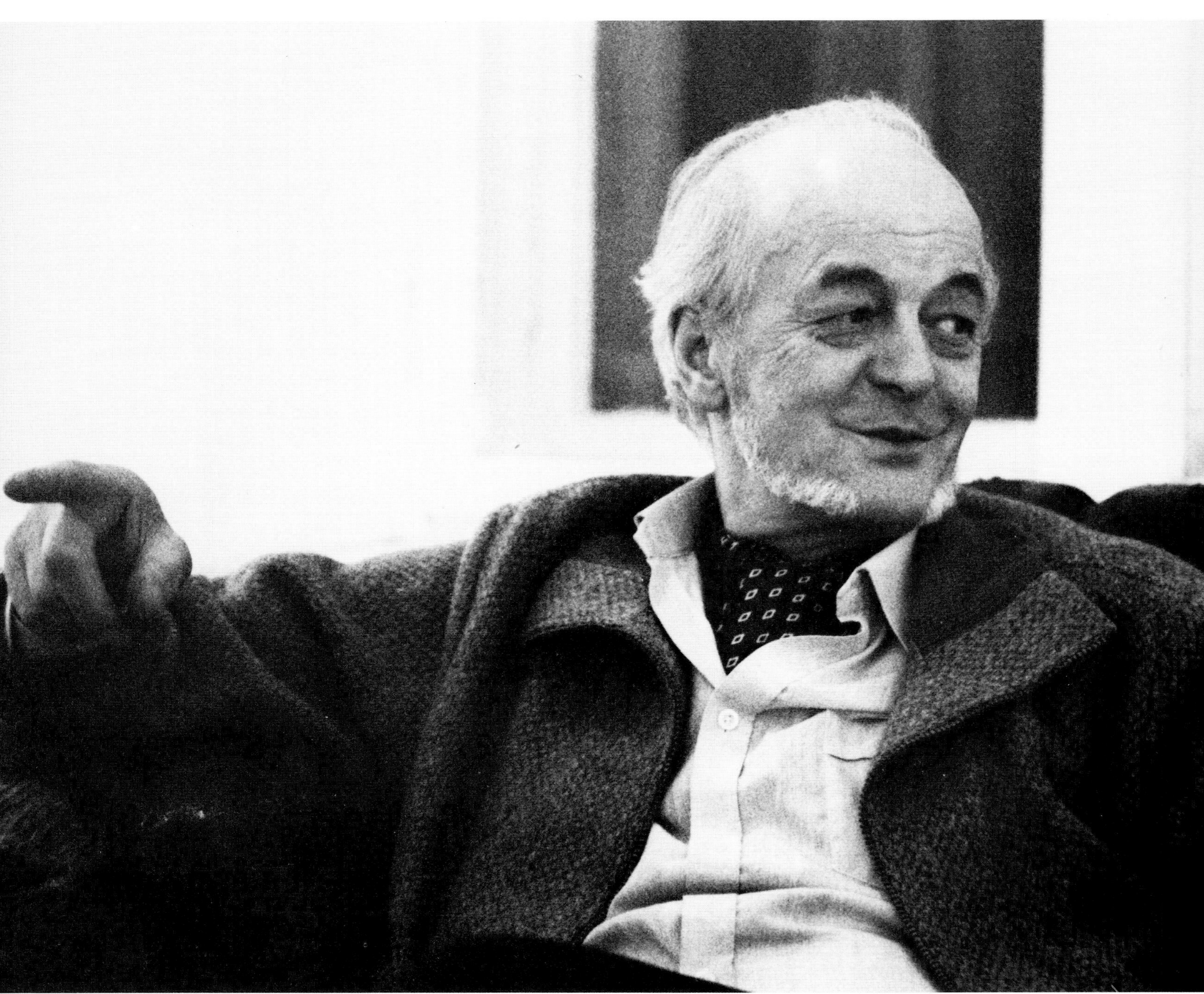

Photograph of the artist, 1983.

Contents

Preface
Douglas G. Schultz — 4

Acknowledgments
Susan Krane — 5

Artist's Statement — 6

Jan Kotik: Other Dimensions
Susan Krane — 7

Remarks on the Works of Jan Kotik
Hans-Peter Riese — 21

Catalogue of the Exhibition — 45

Chronology — 47

Selected Exhibitions — 48

Selected Bibliography — 51

Public Collections — 52

Preface

The work of Jan Kotik has been exhibited widely and with acclaim for over four decades, in both his native Czechoslovakia and throughout Western Europe, yet it has been seen only rarely in this country. The current exhibition is the first comprehensive showing of Kotik's paintings in the United States and is testimony to the maturity and enduring strength of his artistic vision.

Kotik's recent paintings—the focus of this exhibition—are subtle, painterly expressions that illuminate the constant and fertile interrelationship of post-war European and American art, exclusive of the sways of the gallery system and art criticism. Kotik brings to his work a sensitivity for and a love of materials, which is reflected in his evocative handling of paint and color. This he combines with a firm commitment to the anti-illusionistic aesthetics of Minimal and Conceptual art. The result is painting that nourishes the senses as well as the intellect.

Within the universal terms of abstraction, Kotik provokes us to reconsider established notions of painting as static and rarified, without forsaking the traditional textural and sensuous qualities of the medium. At a time when Neo-Expressionism is much heralded, often for its sometimes indulgent extremes, the emotive forces in Kotik's work appear uniquely poised.

I am grateful to Jan Kotik for his generous cooperation with us during all phases of this endeavor. I thank also Susan Krane, Curator, for her skillful organization of the exhibition.

We thank the Berlin Senate for Scientific and Cultural Affairs for their generous support of this exhibition.

Douglas G. Schultz
Director

Acknowledgments

Numerous colleagues and friends of the artist have assisted enthusiastically with the organization of this exhibition. Their generous support has been invaluable.

Marina Dinkler of Galerie Marina Dinkler, West Berlin, aided with the many mundane details of transportation and catalogue preparation. Her cheerful support has facilitated the realization of this project. I am deeply grateful to Charlotta and Petr Kotik for their continual encouragement, friendship and assistance. Their help has been crucial, from the inception of the project, down to the final proofing of unfamiliar Czech names in the catalogue. I also thank Robert T. Buck, former Director of the Albright-Knox Art Gallery, for his initiation and support of the exhibition.

Many of the pieces in the exhibition have been culled from the collection of the artist who, with undue patience, gave us access to his holdings. Steven and Cecile Biltekoff, Monika Babackova, and private collectors made the exhibition possible by the loan of their works. We thank them for their generous cooperation.

I am indebted to the staff of the Albright-Knox Art Gallery. I thank Douglas G. Schultz, Director, for his advice and support. Robert Evren, Researcher, carefully compiled the exhibitions history and bibliography and assisted with numerous other details. Others who worked in particular on the exhibition are: Mary Bell, Assistant Librarian; Bette Blum, Coordinator of Public Relations; Cheryl Brutvan, Assistant Curator of Prints and Drawings; Christine Daniels, Administrative Secretary; Georgette Hasiotis, Editor of Publications; David Kempf, Engineer; Ida Koch, Curatorial Secretary; John Kushner, Building Superintendent; Annette Masling, Librarian; Peter Muscato, Installer; Alba Priore, Assistant Registrar; Serena Rattazzi, Assistant to the Director for Administration; John Small, Maintenance; Daisy Stroud, Assistant to the Building Superintendent; Sarah Ulen, Registrar; Zbynek Jonak, Installer. I also wish to thank David L. Vierlung, translator of the artist's statement, and Larry Fischer, translator of Hans-Peter Riese's essay.

Michael Glass of Michael Glass Design, Inc., designed the catalogue with great sensitivity.

Our sincere thanks go to Hans-Peter Riese for his thoughtful and intelligent essay, which contributes so much to our understanding of Kotik's art.

I am grateful to the artist for generously sharing his gentle wisdom and expansive ideas, despite the oftentimes humorous constraints of language barriers. The singularity and commitment with which Kotik has pursued his art throughout years of great political and social turmoil are examples for us all. For Jan Kotik, art is not simply a profession but an all-encompassing philosophy of life—one that is firmly grounded in the tradition of European humanism yet tempered by an interest in the timeless and selfless qualities of Oriental thought. I thank Jan and Ruth Kotik for their cooperation with all aspects of this exhibition, their hospitality, and the pleasure of working with them.

Susan Krane
Curator

Artist's Statement

During the restoration of the St. Vitus Cathedral in Prague in the forties, I had an opportunity to climb up onto the scaffolding to study the architectural details. I found the tiny cornices, branches and reliefs, which were only really visible from this vantage point, to be of a beauty equal—if not superior—to those things which could be viewed from below. This experience was an important lesson for me. It taught me the importance of seeing a work in its entirety, including those details that are not immediately recognizable, in order to appreciate fully its complexity and honesty.

There are objects or spaces that we see practically daily without really being aware of them in any detail; then suddenly when seen in a particular light, or from a particular perspective, they are revealed to us quite distinctly. They speak to us, they move us deeply.

The innermost feeling of being touched is brought about in me by certain circumstances: spaces which open out from themselves, which close in upon themselves, always forming new spaces, new edges. I have experienced this kind of magic in the *Malà Strana* in Prague [an historic architectural district on the left bank of the Vltava River], in Venice and in certain old cities on the Dalmatian coast. I do not know why these particular spatial combinations (both urban and rural) have this effect on me. Or why it is that, upon seeing them, I suddenly feel so extraordinarily well.

I recall a small building under construction on the Avenue of the Americas in lower Manhattan. It stood on a piece of land that required an unusual architectural treatment, different from the rigid angular approach that predominates in the area. Pieces of the prefabricated slabs of fired brick which were fastened to the bearing wall had come loose, and had begun to disintegrate. Outside and inside of this disintegration a new space was created; it was unique, a breakthrough into the facade, a window, a wide crack for one to see through. Or perhaps it was like bark peeling off a tree, or the roping off of a construction zone, or a conglomeration of functional objects whose forms, colors, letters or significations created a new combination of meanings, quite different from those originally intended. In any case, these were new forms separated from their original functions. Just as when one looks at facades bleached by rain and sun, or the diagonal crosses and wavy lines found on newly installed glass windows, or water puddles, or the dark forms of freshly paved asphalt. All of these things can be, but are not always, intensely poetic in their effect here and now.

I often have the inexplicable urge to transmute one situation into another; to open a crack into the space, to enclose it as naturally as bark covers a tree. That is why I do not like "right angled" painting (i.e. least of all framed pictures); they are at odds with their surroundings, they do not contribute to their surroundings but merely decorate them. I do not like "pure" geometry, nor simple truthfulness of color and gesture, nor plain surfaces, and still less, an illusionary space on the surface.

It has long been maintained that painting should attempt to mirror nature. Perhaps there is some truth in that, for if one compares the process of creating a painting to nature's process of creation, one discovers similar organic origins and transformations.

Jan Kotik: Other Dimensions

Susan Krane

*To all appearances, the artist acts like a mediumistic
being who, from the labyrinth beyond time and
space, seeks his way out to a clearing.*

Marcel Duchamp[1]

The subtle, painterly surfaces and matter-of-fact
geometric formats of Jan Kotik's recent works em-
body a complexity of ideas that their understated
presence at first belies. One soon becomes aware,
however, of the compelling paradoxes that abound
and reverberate within these paintings. The con-
summate rationality of Kotik's relief structures
contrasts with the expressive painterliness of their
surfaces: We perceive simultaneously an imper-
sonal, at times mathematical, control and an intense subjectivity. The orderly definition of the
component parts is pitted against their arbitrary
placement, so that elements of overt playfulness
oppugn a certain refined elegance. With this mul-
tiplicity of factors comes a realm of evocations. Kotik's seemingly simple, finite forms speak of infinite
variations, of order and of chaos. The works have
an enigmatic metaphorical resonance and meditative aura.

The discordancies inherent in Jan Kotik's
painting may initially seem incompatible, particularly for American audiences perhaps accustomed
to a more pragmatic and absolute artistic vision.
For example, both the concise form and the gestural brushwork of Kotik's art appear familiar:
They provoke immediate associations with the dis-
parate and seemingly irreconcilable aesthetic attitudes of, respectively, Minimal art and Abstract
Expressionism. It is important, however, that Kotik's art did not originate as a dialectical response
—as a direct, adamant answer to the art that has
come before it—as did that of many of the American artists with which his art has immediate visual
parallels. The polarities within Kotik's work, then,
need not be considered problematic contradictions. For him, dissonance is rather a means of
creating a dialogue between various perceptual
faculties. Jan Kotik's work reveals itself through
incongruities; it is about possibilities rather than
resolutions.

Kotik has undeniable sympathies with aspects
of Minimal and Conceptual art (on which have
often been placed solidly American claims). Yet, at
the age of sixty-eight, he is a generation older than
many of the artists with whom he shares a concern
for the sheer physicality or intellectual origins of

the art object. His mature work has evolved quite
independently, and is rooted primarily in his experiences in post-war Europe. His cultural heritage
and the complex political circumstances in which
he has grown have molded the foundations of his
art.

. . . .

Kotik was born in 1916 in Turnov, Bohemia, which
was shortly to become part of Czechoslovakia after
the dissolution of the Austro-Hungarian Empire.
He spent his childhood near Prague, Kafka's city
of haunting baroque splendor. With the formation
of the republic, Prague soon became a cosmopoli-
tan cultural center which maintained close ties to
Paris as well as Vienna. Its rich artistic life flour-
ished on the strong foundations of the earlier
Jugendstil and Symbolist art in the city. Later,
many progressive exhibitions of modern art were
held there: for example, a major show of Edvard
Munch paintings in 1905; an exhibition of works
by the Impressionists, van Gogh and Cézanne in
1907; a selection of work from the 1910 Salon des
Indépendants (including pieces by Matisse, Derain
and Vlaminck) and an exhibition in 1913 of Cubism, Orphism, Futurism.[2]

Indigenous activity was somewhat stronger in
music, poetry and literature than in the visual arts,
yet there were continuous artistic ties to the Parisian avant-garde through František Kupka and
others.[3] In 1920, for example, a traveling Dada
tour visited Prague. Although it met with great resistance (in part a nationalistic Czech reaction to
the German origin of the work), Schwitters and
Hausmann nonetheless organized a poetry reading and *Merz* soirée in Prague the following year.[4]
Also of major importance was the visibility of the
collection of the art historian Dr. Vincenc Kramář,
director of the Picture Gallery of the Society of Pa-
triotic Patrons of Art in Prague from 1919 to 1939.
Kramář had amassed major holdings of works by
Picasso, Rousseau, Derain, Braque and others
when he lived in Paris.[5] His acquisitions for the
Gallery were progressive as well and he was instru-
mental in making available to Czech artists prime
examples of School of Paris modernism.

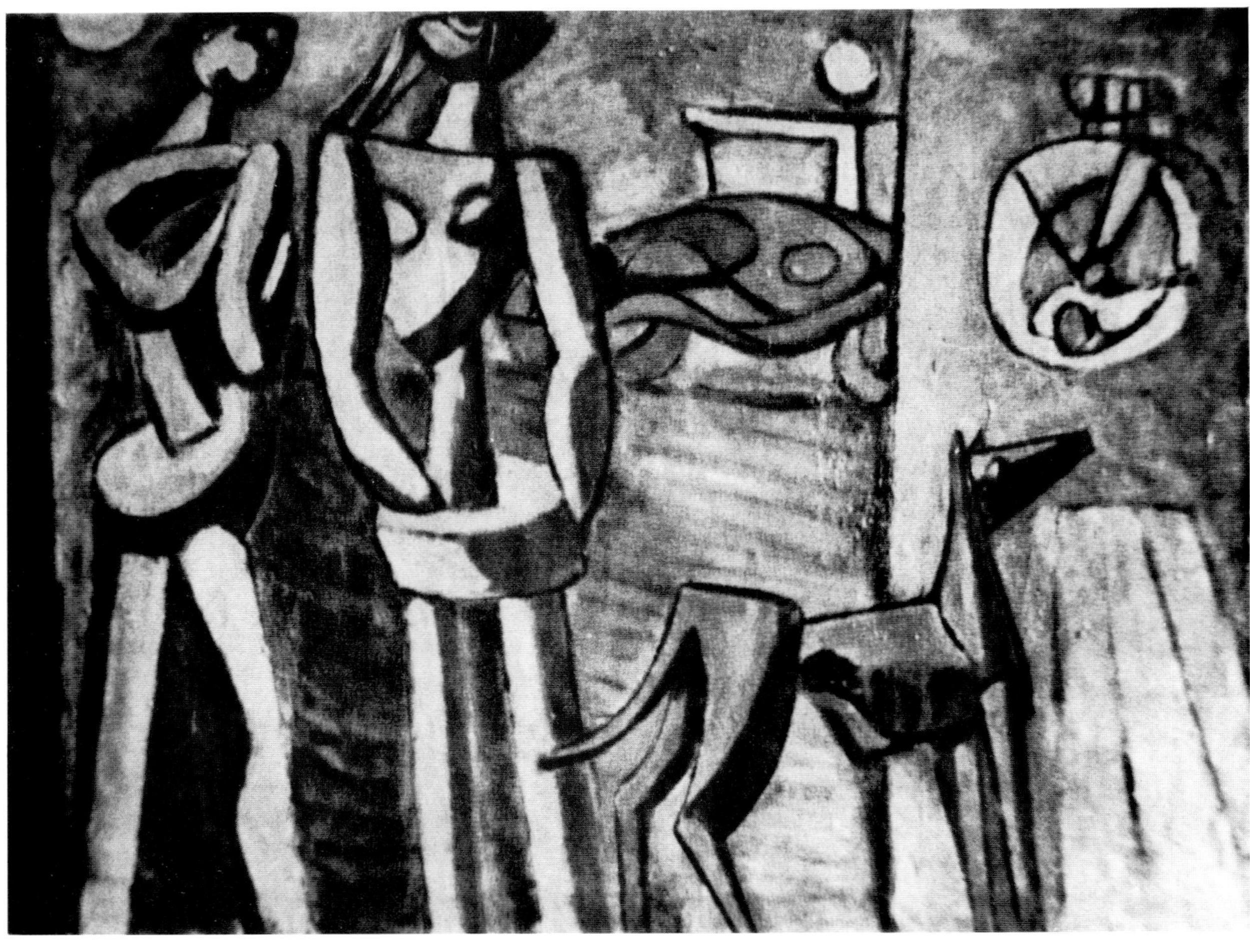

Street, 1940-41, oil on canvas, 27¾ x 43½". Collection Středočeská Galerie, Roudnice, Czechoslovakia.

Through his father, the well-known Czech Cubist painter Pravoslov Kotik, Jan Kotik became acquainted early on with the international avant-garde movements that had thrived before the war, as well as with native Czech Cubism, the mystical abstractions of Kupka, Surrealism and the melancholic and poetic variations of the active Prague surrealist contingent.

During his twenties, Kotik painted works that were figurative and in a Cubist idiom, although their content was often tinged with a surreal psychological dislocation. His career was abruptly interrupted by Hitler's occupation of Czechoslovakia in 1939. Life changed drastically with the upheavals and disasters of the war years, and the concomitant imposition of artistic prohibitions. Contact with the outside world was severely limited, and Kotik and others of the avant-garde were eventually forbidden to exhibit their art.

In 1942, in the midst of the occupation, Kotik together with other artists, poets and writers formed *Gruppe 42*[6], a loose association whose members shared the commitment that art must reflect modern urban life, "not the *art world* in

which we live, but rather the *world* in which we live."[7] For the visual artists, this meant addressing themselves to subjects of routine daily life. They often filled these scenes with symbolism that reflected the intense anxieties and political tensions of the time. The aims of the group were, in the most general terms, humanistic, and were influenced as well by socialist and Marxist sympathies then common among the European intelligentsia and artistic circles, particularly in the face of rising fascist regimes.

For a brief period following the end of World War II in 1945, there were increased opportunities for travel and exhibitions. Kotik and his associates "tried to make up for lost time." He had his first one-artist exhibition and, with other young Czech artists, was included in exhibitions throughout Europe. In 1946, Kotik journeyed to Finland and Paris, where he remained for two months. There he recalls seeing Dubuffet's early, crude paintings at Galerie René Drouin (the exhibition of which was widely heralded as a *succès de scandale*). In Prague, however, Surrealism remained dominant, fueled by the showing of an exhibition from Paris

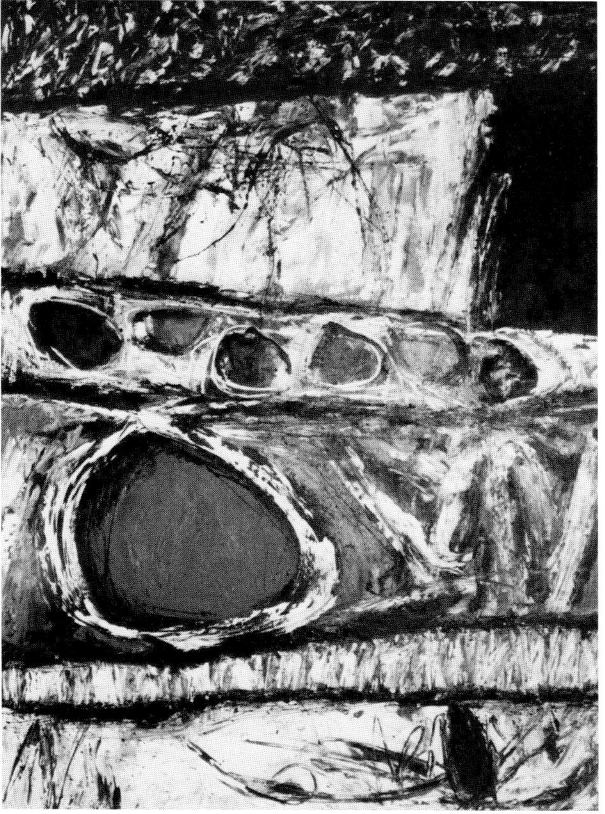

Untitled, 1961, oil on canvas, 51¼ x 38⅛". Collection of the artist.

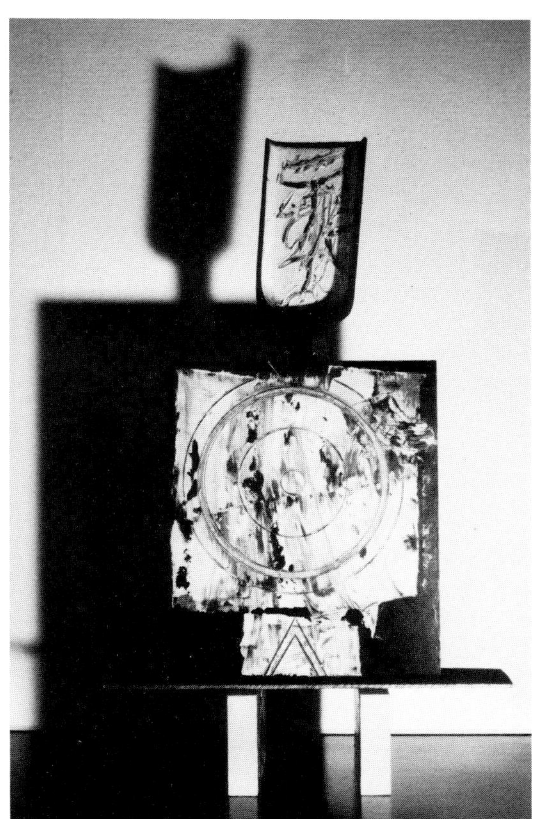

Untitled, 1961, oil on wood, oil on canvas, wood, 25½ x 15¾ x 8". Collection of the artist.

in 1947;[8] the establishment of *Gruppe RA*, a Surrealist organization active from 1946 to 1948;[9] and André Breton's visit in 1947 to what he called "the magic capital of Europe."[10]

This momentum and burgeoning internationalism were abruptly halted with the advent of the communist regime in 1948. Artistic liberties were sharply curtailed and Social Realism was deemed the only permissible style, a situation to which few artists in *Gruppe 42* could accommodate themselves. Many of the younger artists, including Kotik, could hardly go along with this authoritarian dictate, which had seriously disaffected their socialist ideals. Kotik's art was considered "formalist—degenerate art," and he was again forbidden to sell or exhibit his work.

Kotik continued to paint in isolation but was employed in graphics, industrial design and glassmaking, an art form with a rich tradition in Czechoslovakia. It was a difficult time for him, without artistic interaction:

> *…I was a 'forbidden' painter who couldn't show his work; the police actions had somehow become more refined than they were under the Nazis and more efficient, and that led to a basic fear within the populace to even communicate or to talk with one another without feeling that it was somehow being used.*

Over the course of the early fifties, Kotik became dissatisfied with the style of his painting and gradually resolved to "somehow deconstruct all the post-Cubist structures I had been working with, destroy them with the idea that by doing this I would be coming closer to a pure abstract art." He experimented with various means, such as Surrealist techniques of automatic drawing, and with calligraphy. Fascinated by the free-flowing graphic quality of Chinese calligraphy, Kotik tried to emulate the gestural movements in India ink paintings of animals. These exercises were liberating for him. By the mid-fifties, Kotik, with no information of artistic developments in the outside world, was working in a loosely gestural manner with heavily impastoed surfaces.

These comparatively small-sized canvases retained vestiges of figural elements and biomorphic shapes. For Kotik, whether the works were figurative or not was irrelevant. The primary issue for him was that the paintings had an inner dynamic that corresponded more closely to the vitality of the human world than had his rigid, Cubist-derived descriptive paintings. This turn from the mimetic approach of his figurative work to the analogous evocation of reality through what was dubbed "imaginative expressionism" marked an important step in Kotik's aesthetic thinking. By destroying pictorial order, he was striving to establish a direct correspondence between the spontaneous actions of the painter and the similarly organic, "independent order" of human life and nature.[11]

Not surprisingly, this major transformation in Kotik's art and in the terms of his humanistic approach had close affinities with contemporaneous efforts of the Abstract Expressionists in America and, in Europe, the *tachistes*, the Cobra artists, Tàpies and Dubuffet. They held in common their search for pictorial immediacy and for means of expressing the mythic and the universal in man's inner, primal experiences. Widespread was the desire to transcend the profane, everyday world, in which faith had been immeasurably shaken by the recent unfathomable catastrophes of a war that had rent apart the realities of life and civilization.

These artistic parallels surprised Kotik when he first re-established contact with foreign artists. After the death of Stalin in 1953, life gradually became a bit freer and foreign periodicals were occasionally available. In September of 1956, Kotik was able to travel to Alba, Italy to attend the conference of MIBI, the "Mouvement international pour un Bauhaus imaginiste" [International Union for a Pictorial Bauhaus], whose chief participants were Asger Jorn, Pinot Gallizio, Constant, Gil Wolman and Enrico Baj. Pravoslav Rada and Kotik arrived from Czechoslovakia near the end of the congress and added their names to the statement drawn up by the others.[12] The group was a short-lived coalition of various existing associations of artists, poets, writers and architects such as the *Lettrist* group based in Paris and *Movimento Nucleare*. While MIBI had no firm doctrine, many members were critical of bourgeois society from a more or less Marxist standpoint. Internationalism and a total amalgamation of various artistic media were espoused through participatory art, such as public "spectacles," visionary urban planning and non-illusionistic painting that addressed spatial issues.[13] The visual artists in particular were gathered in their opposition to the cool abstractions of Max Bill's "New Bauhaus" [*Hochschule für Gestaltung*]

in Ulm. They called instead for active images that reflected contact with the vitality and "combustion" of life, and for experiments in "psychogeography" —the primal territory of the subconscious.[14]

The conference was important for Kotik not so much for the polemics and inflated theorizing, but primarily because it provided an affirmation of the direction in which he had moved independently. Crucial to his thinking also was his contact in Alba with the Danish artist Asger Jorn, a founder of Cobra. Jorn, like Kotik, had been unable to travel or exhibit during the years of Nazi occupation and had then, through experimentation with Surrealist automatism and his interest in Nordic myths and folk art, developed his dense, vibrantly-colored abstractions.[15] At the time of their meeting, Cobra artists had long since disbanded. Jorn had recently been dividing his time between Paris and Albisola, Italy, where he worked on ceramics at the Mazzotti factory along with, among others, Appel, Baj, Corneille, Fontana and Matta, and at the same time pursued his spontaneous, gestural works.[16] This dialogue with Jorn reaffirmed Kotik's proclivities, as did later sporadic knowledge (primarily through catalogues and periodicals) of the works of Tàpies, Burri and Fontana.

By the early sixties, artistic opportunities increased dramatically in Czechoslovakia. With the easing of the political situation, Kotik's critical discourses were published with increasing frequency in various periodicals. Firm and outspoken in his commitments, Kotik became an important figure for Czech avant-garde painters. When international art critics like Dore Ashton and Pierre Restany began to visit Prague, it was often Kotik who was their guide. They found much of the work overly derivative, and many of the Czech artists, in Ashton's words, "pathetically conscientious in their extremism."[17] Yet, they noted the surprising and unprecedented vitality of the small but hearty Czech avant-garde.

. . . .

For Kotik, the immediacy of *tachisme* or *art informel* shortly proved too much of an "amorphous protoplasm,"[18] too nebulous and inhumane. It became increasingly clear to him that in order for his painting to be in direct relationship with reality, it physically had to "leave the wall" as he had written in a notation as early as 1952.[19] Later, in the sixties, he experimented with various ways of "bringing real space into painting." These efforts included

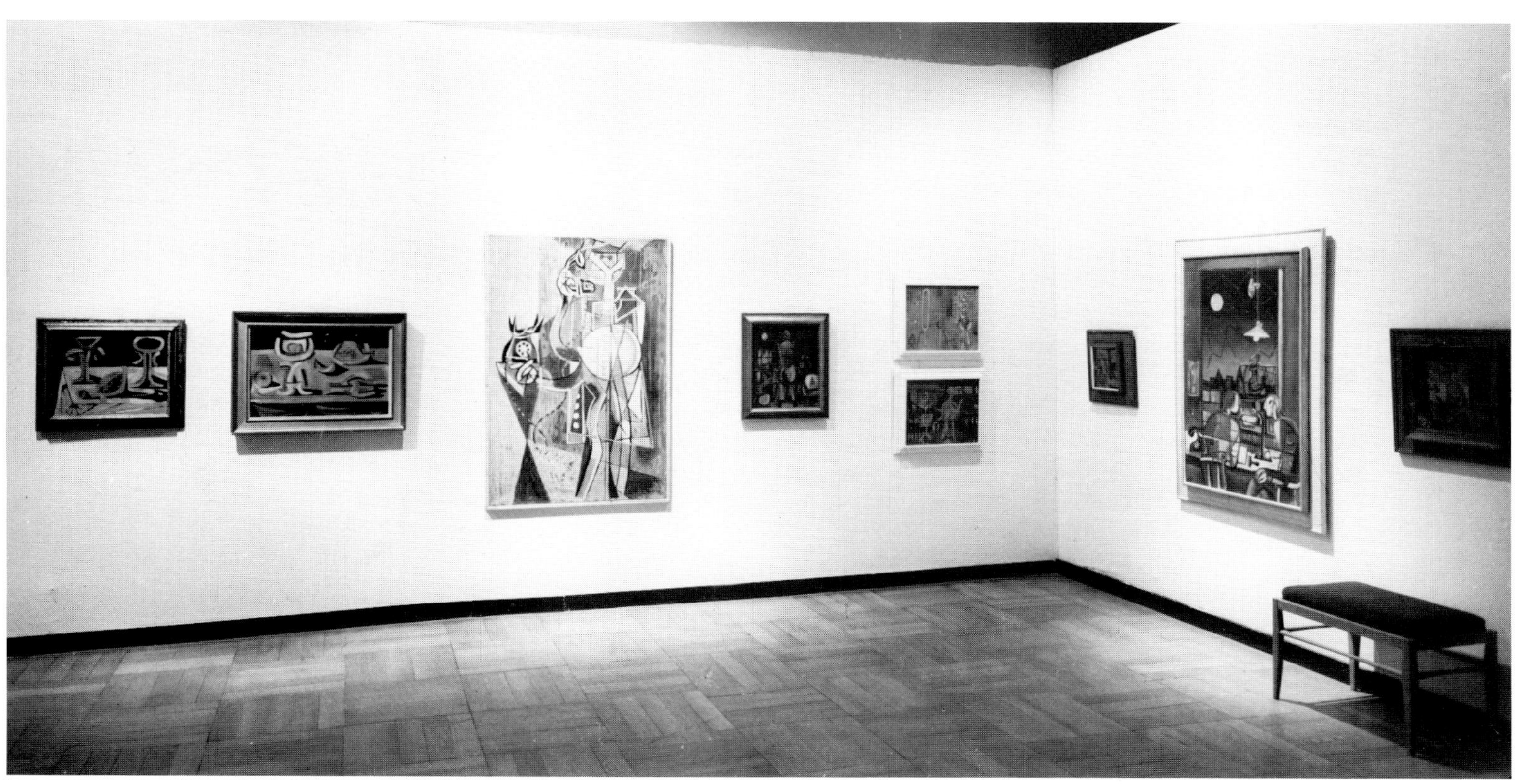

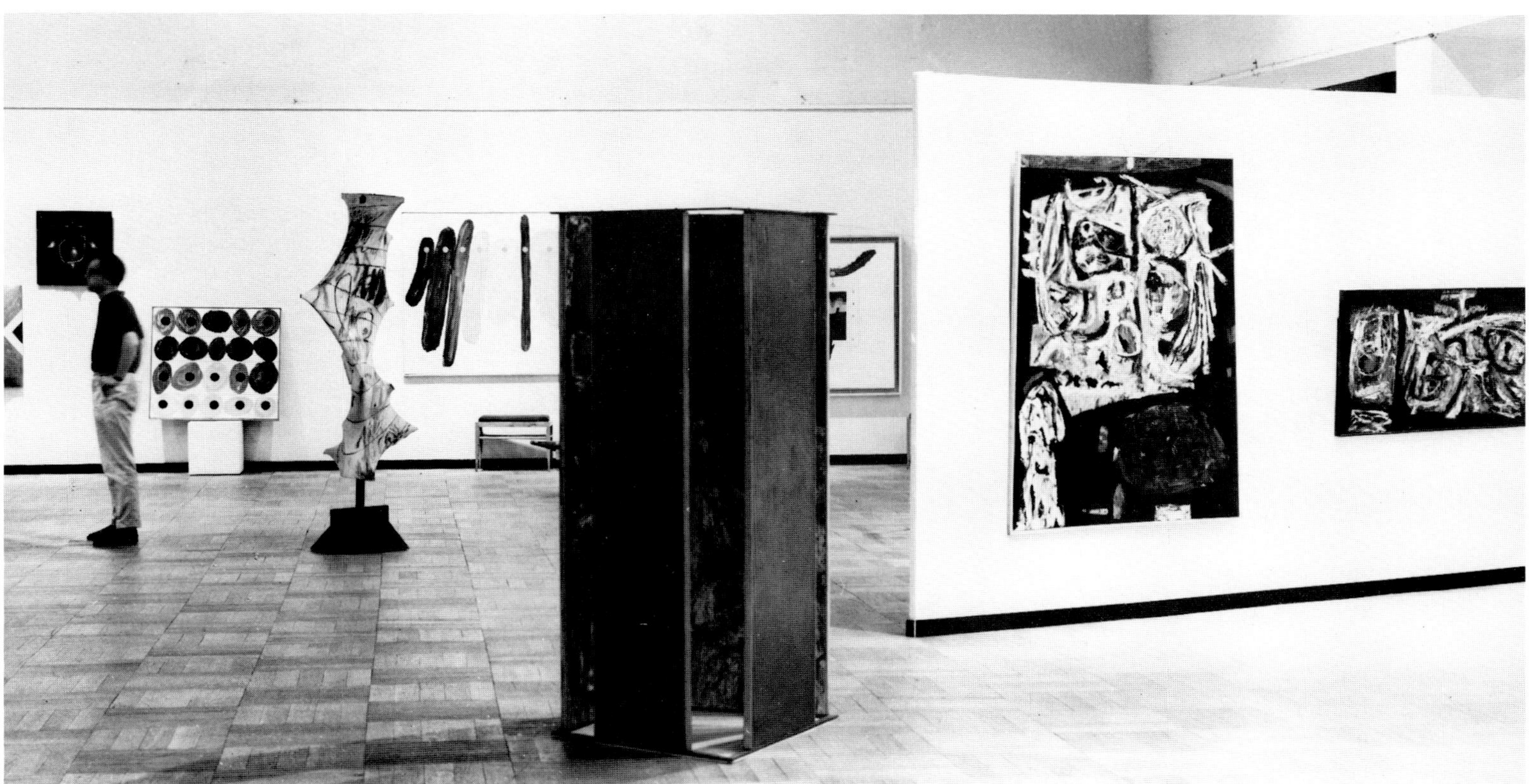

Installation views of *Jan Kotík: 1939-1968*, Výstavní síň Mánes,
Prague, 1968.

three-dimensional painted assemblages, constructions of movable painted panels suspended like a screen, and (at the end of the decade) eccentric canvases stretched tightly over protrusions or free-standing armatures. Rather than working with the psychological space of the painting's surface, Kotik turned to the possibility of working with aggressive physical space.

At the heart of Kotik's mature work have been this exploration of spatial issues and attempt to integrate painting, as an object, into our physical reality. His work has not evolved in a strict linear fashion but rather, in Kotik's words, like a continuous spiral. He finds himself discovering familiar ideas in guises of formal variations. Since his emigration to West Berlin in 1969, Kotik's work has assumed a number of forms: paintings (more specifically, painted objects or relief constructions) divided into component shapes that open out or are hung with interstices between them; installations incorporating elements drawn on the wall, objects hung on the wall and, often times, projecting elements; systemic projects; and free-hanging canvas pieces. Endemic to all is Kotik's belief that "the picture is not a projection screen: the spatial should not be illusionistic."[20] As he explains:

> I was always unhappy and disappointed with the notion of art as some type of decoration that hangs on a wall. The question that always came up was what can you do to change that? What can happen to the picture? Naturally this comes from the tradition of Cubism. In the beginning of Cubism there was also this attempt to go from the image to the object—somehow.

Along with this overtly materialistic stance came a desire to burst open the frame that held the painting in its ethereal realm. This Kotik took to an anti-aesthetic end point as he strove "to connect painting to the spatial situation in which it is exhibited in a real room, real space."

Kotik's means (as for many Minimalist sculptors of the same period) was to emphasize and define space by creating relationships between the objects within a field of vision. For example, in a painting such as *Untitled*, 1980 (cat. 15, ill. p. 35), Kotik accentuates the three-dimensionality of the work by means of the gap opened between its elements, the irregular perimeter, and by hanging the top element from a chain. He points as well to the exposed space on the wall, to the distinction between the plane of the wall and that of the canvas, and to that between the linear edge of the components and the line of charcoal traversing their surfaces. Like the gravitational tug of a horizon line,

the painted piece of wood on which the elements are set both visually anchors the work and gives the elements above a contrasting buoyancy.

When discussing his notion of space, Kotik is fond of citing a verse from the Lao-tzu:

> *Moulding clay into a vessel, we find the utility in its hollowness;*
> *Cutting doors and windows for a house, we find the utility in its empty space.*
> *Therefore the being of things is profitable, the non-being of things is serviceable.*[21]

The chapter illustrates for him the potency of empty or negative space, which Kotik seeks to activate. In his constructions, the placement of forms serves to make the space articulate, to make it "become matter."

Kotik's concepts of space, as well as other aspects of his thinking, have indeed been shaped by his interest and readings in Oriental philosophy. Many of his polemical writings and statements on his work echo the influences of Taoist thought. "The most important thing in empty spaces is emptiness," he has written. "If one succeeds in heightening and intensifying this emptiness, there is quiet and peace."[22] It is in these aspects that Kotik's recent work goes beyond being a mere exercise in visual perception and assumes a humanistic, spiritual content (as had his representational work and the *informel* abstractions of the late fifties). This romantic, expressive essence greatly distinguishes even the most reductive of Kotik's work from the cool and calculated statements of Minimal art, particularly the work of artists such as Richard Serra, Robert Mangold or Robert Morris.

The component parts of Kotik's work, and in particular his recent multi-part paintings, often have a functional rather than compositional look that is in part a result of their hinged or suspended arrangements. This functionalism implies performance of movement and, with that, infinite permutations of form.

This evocation of transformation is integral to Kotik's art. Works such as the early *Objet transformable [Transformable Object]*, 1972-73, (cat. 1, ill. p. 25) are meant to be casually arranged and rearranged like an intriguing puzzle, each new configuration revealing different compositions of color and modulations in the surface of the relief. Kotik in fact occasionally exhibited alongside this piece (and others) photographs of some of its various arrangements to override the "do-not-touch" constraints of public exhibitions. A similar, though less specific, sense of transformation exists in his free-hanging linen works from the mid-seventies:

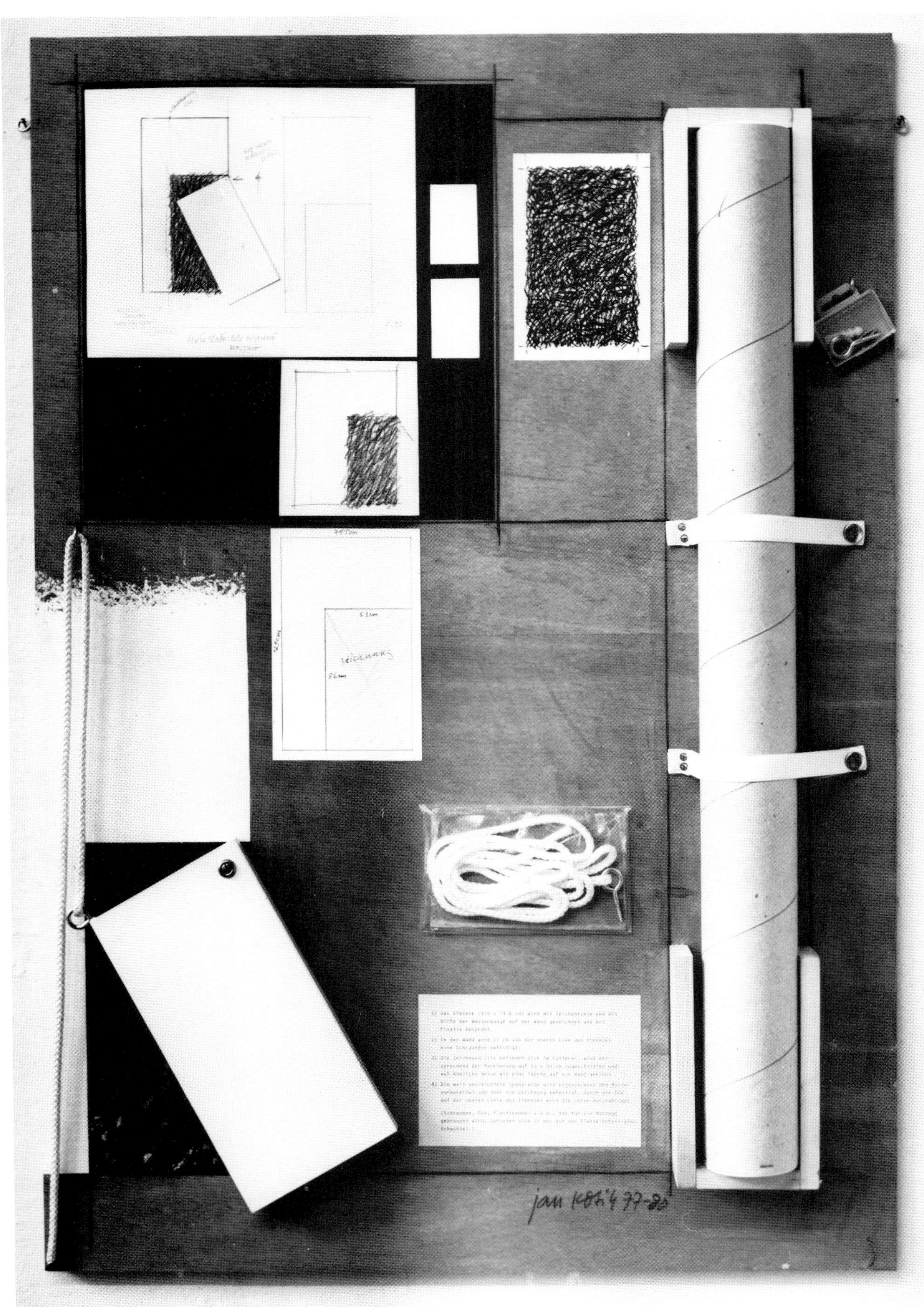

Untitled, 1977-80, assemblage, 39½ x 27½". Collection of the artist.

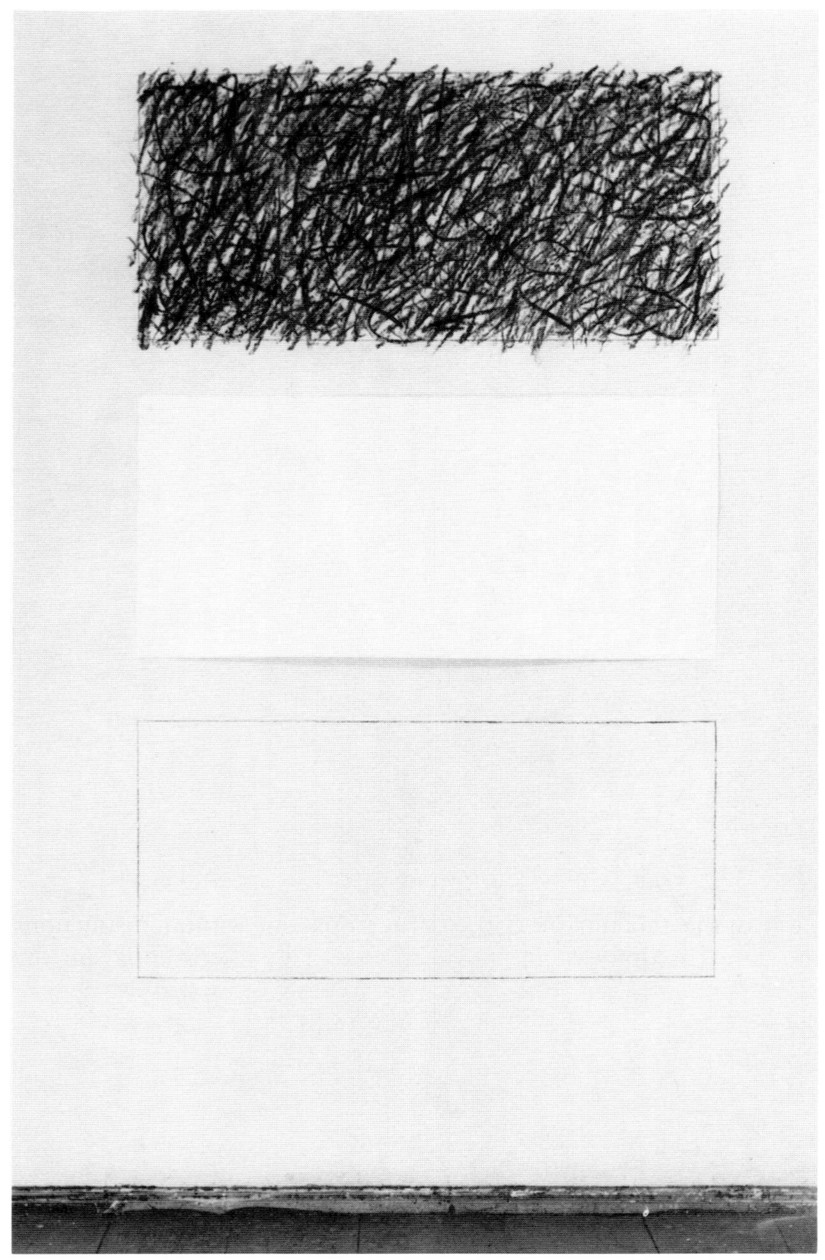

Fig. 1. Installation for *28 Jahresausstellungen des Deutschen Kunstlerbundes*, Kunstverein, Hanover, West Germany, 1980. Charcoal wall drawing and paper.

these appear casually hung, their forms subject to the dictates of gravity and the process of their making embodied in their appearance.

In the late sixties, Kotik became increasingly dissatisfied with the fact that his works often looked unconditionally fixed and static.[23] He was interested not in art with specific content, but in work that metamorphosed either internally or through an external change in context, and thus obtained different meanings with each new situation.[24] By making objects that could be transposed, Kotik felt he could express even in finished forms the flux of the process of artistic creation. The work, endowed with a continual possibility for growth, in turn reflected the organic process of creation in nature:

> *In a certain sense, the work of art has a parallel to nature—in the sense that it develops or grows in the same way as a natural thing, like a tree.*

Kotik's desire to imbue these spare forms with vestiges of their making, and thus to symbolize the organic cycles of nature, is consistent with the intentions of his abstractions of the fifties. In spite of the contemporary look of his latest work, Kotik's art and his philosophies are firmly rooted in this earlier era of modernism. He remains close in spirit to the Abstract Expressionists. Whereas

Jackson Pollock could go as far as declaring "I am nature," Kotik's spiritual stance is more transcendental than heroic and perhaps in this respect more quintessentially European.

A work like *Untitled*, 1980 (cat. 37, ill. p. 43) with its selected configurations of crumpled and torn paper, is not purely an epistemological statement about art, as is true for much of the Conceptual art with which his work has often been compared. Rather, the intent of this modest piece is ontological: Understood in the context of Kotik's oeuvre it is like a parable, indicative of the continuous nature of being and reality.

Kotik's concept of reality as ephemeral and non-linear, yet endlessly mutable, is clearly related again to Orientalism and especially Taoism. What is important for Kotik is not the goal of a finished work, but what one discovers along the path of its creation. He believes that "We know the direction we are going in but we have no idea what our destination will be." Moreover, if one actively seeks an end, or follows a desire, one rarely obtains it. Instead the artist, as an individual, must remain open to serendipitous discovery. Such statements reflect basic elements of the way of the Tao, mirrored in such verses as "He who stands on tiptoe is not steady. He who strides forward does not go."[25]

Kotik is firm in his beliefs but gentle-spoken. He has long committed himself to following his own direction, perhaps both because and in spite of the great adversities he has encountered. He cares little about the reaction of the public or critics, not at all about sales, and scorns the marketplace atmosphere and glitter of the art world. He continues to work diligently, in relative solitude. The attitudes he voices about being an artist, with a certain self-abnegation and suppression of conscious will, correspond closely to the teachings of Lao-tzu:

> *All things arise, and he does not turn away from them. He produces them but does not take possession of them. He acts but does not rely on his own ability. He accomplishes his task but does not claim credit that his accomplishment remains with him.*[26]

Many of the subtleties and the apparent contradictions of Kotik's work can be better understood, too, in the light of the Tao's illustrations by negation and contradiction. Regarding one work (fig. 1, ill. at left), Kotik says, "I'm not interested, for instance, in the similarities of these objects but rather the dissimilarities in variations of the same." Through understated distinctions, Kotik emphasizes the specific essence of each part and the totality of the whole, "to show that the same is not the same." Thus the poetic contrasts, for instance, between a line drawn on the wall and one drawn on the canvas become for the artist an index of an intangible reality, one that is always changing yet ever the same.

Kotik has assimilated aspects of Oriental thought in a general sense—one that is extracted from its cultural context and compatible with his ingrained European intellectual background and artistic proclivities. For instance, he illustrates his conviction that an art object is not intrinsically precious, but rather an object just as any other object, by pointing to a Chinese work he owns which is nothing more or less than a beautiful slab of green marble, elegantly framed and signed. The inflections of Kotik's philosophical interests are evident perhaps only on this theoretical level. They are reflected in the work itself as a provocative but nebulous, meditative quality.

It seems natural, given Kotik's interest in philosophical abstractions, that the concept of time has been of recurring importance in his work. Most basically, time takes on a mythical dimension for Kotik, one without distinctions or linear sequence. This all-encompassing, interpenetrating continuity is echoed in the physical variability of Kotik's objects: They carry implications of their transformation ad infinitum.

During the mid-seventies, the temporal dimension of art became of increasing interest to Kotik. He focused specifically on conveying a sense of ritualistic time—the sense of removal from ordinary time and events which seems inherent to our experience of all pictorial art. In works such as *objekt für sieben wochentage [Object for Seven Days of the Week]*, 1974-75, objekt für normale und für besondere tage [Object for Normal and Special Days], 1975, (both shown at the Venice Biennale in 1976) and *objekt für vier jahreszeiten [Object for Four Seasons]*, 1975, Kotik attempted to relate ritualistic time to "human time." He established a direct correspondence between the work and the rhythms of daily life. For example, *Jahresobjekt [Year's Object]*, an installation at Amerika Haus in West Berlin in 1975, consisted of 365 moveable poles, every seventh one colored. Viewers were to move one a day, thus participating in the "ritual," transforming the object, and "visualizing time." Of equal importance for Kotik was the communal nature of these pieces. The ritual activity instigated by the work was a means of creating what he calls "conviviality:"

In these universal terms, Kotik's art retains
the moral and political foundations first evident in
his early scenes of urban life from the *Gruppe 42*
years. Yet Kotik eschews the idea that art can or
should be connected with specific political ideolo-
gies. Victimized by Nazi attacks on avant-garde art
and subsequent Soviet purges of formalism as
"evil," Kotik holds that "the mixture of politics and
art leads to nothing…it brings no artistic results.
We have learned that." Of his early work, he de-
clared "the art work was not apolitical but rather
anti-political and for life, in the sense of life going
on without politics." His discussions of his work
have distinct and strongly humanistic underpin-
nings, although Kotik asserts that he gives no consideration to the viewer's reactions or to the works
"accessibility."

Kotik maintains that art is an inextricably
necessary aspect of human society, yet he stands in
opposition to the detached "art for art's sake" atti-
tude pervasive among many formalists, and to
populist art movements as well. He has written:

> It has become fashionable to demand the social en-
> gagement of art. One could just as well ask a fish to
> swim.…
>
> Let us stay with the fish. It is supposed to swim;
> [suppose] the liquid which is recommended for it
> is like vitriol. Only a very frustrated fish will be
> persuaded to follow this recommendation. They
> demand that art should serve society. Art serves it
> anyway; in a way similar to that in which lungs
> serve man: but it does not "wait on" man and is not
> "at anyone's disposal" like a servant.[30]

Contributing to the complexities of Kotik's
particular humanistic commitment are many factors, not the least of them being the socialist and
Marxist political foundation of the war years. Indeed, the orientation of many artists after the
formation of the republic of Czechoslovakia was
nationalistic, as they searched for indigenous subjects and a vitality of expression. Kotik's father was
essentially anti-elitist and his paintings were so-
cially oriented, often scenes of daily working life.
Jan Kotik, raised in his father's milieu and trained
primarily in the applied arts, grew up with an understanding of art as an important element in daily
discourse as well as intellectual life. He came to believe staunchly that a painting should not be a rarified object of aesthetic devotion, but must relate

directly and immediately to the real physical world
in which we live, be it through the representational
means of his early paintings or the aggressive physical presence of his mature work.

. . . .

The at time totemic character of Kotik's recent paintings with their changeable forms is a further expression of his probing of reality, literally
and philosophically. "The 'open' work of art is a
manifestation of the open structure of every living
thing; it forces one to be aware of life.… The mental is always borne by the material,"[31] he has explained. This constant dialogue between the
"mental" and the "material" results in numerous
contrasts within his work: between the objectivity
of the geometric forms and the expressive realm of
his painterly surfaces; between geometric space
and atmospheric space; between logical order and
chaos; between the classical and the romantic
spheres. There is, for Kotik, a careful symbiosis at
work here. For instance, the geometric shapes of
the canvases act as a "skeleton," a supporting ar-
mature necessary to anchor the evocative painterly
surface firmly to earthly reality. Through contrast,
the characteristics of each are heightened.

In part, these dualities are an outgrowth of
his working methods. Kotik paints with a certain
spontaneous abandon, working many layers of
paint over the canvas until he achieves a subtle lu-
minescence and dynamic interaction of color, and
the indefinable aura of "feeling" in the work. He
has a traditional craftsman's respect and love for
his medium—the sensuous materiality of paint,
the intrinsic characteristics of the canvas. He con-
ceives of the creative process as an essential "part-
nership" between the artist and his materials:

> If one denies the nature of the material, the work
> of art seems artificial and therefore also unbelieva-
> ble. One wants to create objects which are real, con-
> crete matters-of-course, which are like nature.[32]

Kotik is in effect rhapsodic about this communion:

> I've always been convinced that the direct work-
> ings between the artist and his material (reflected)
> a very deep truth underlying a civilization and
> people. When I talk about working with a paint-
> ing, I don't simply mean working with a paint
> brush in a pictorial sense.… It's a part of life, this
> working with material.

This painterly activity is preceded however
by numerous careful studies, mock-ups and
sketches in various media. Some are exactingly
ruled, almost architectural draftings, in which

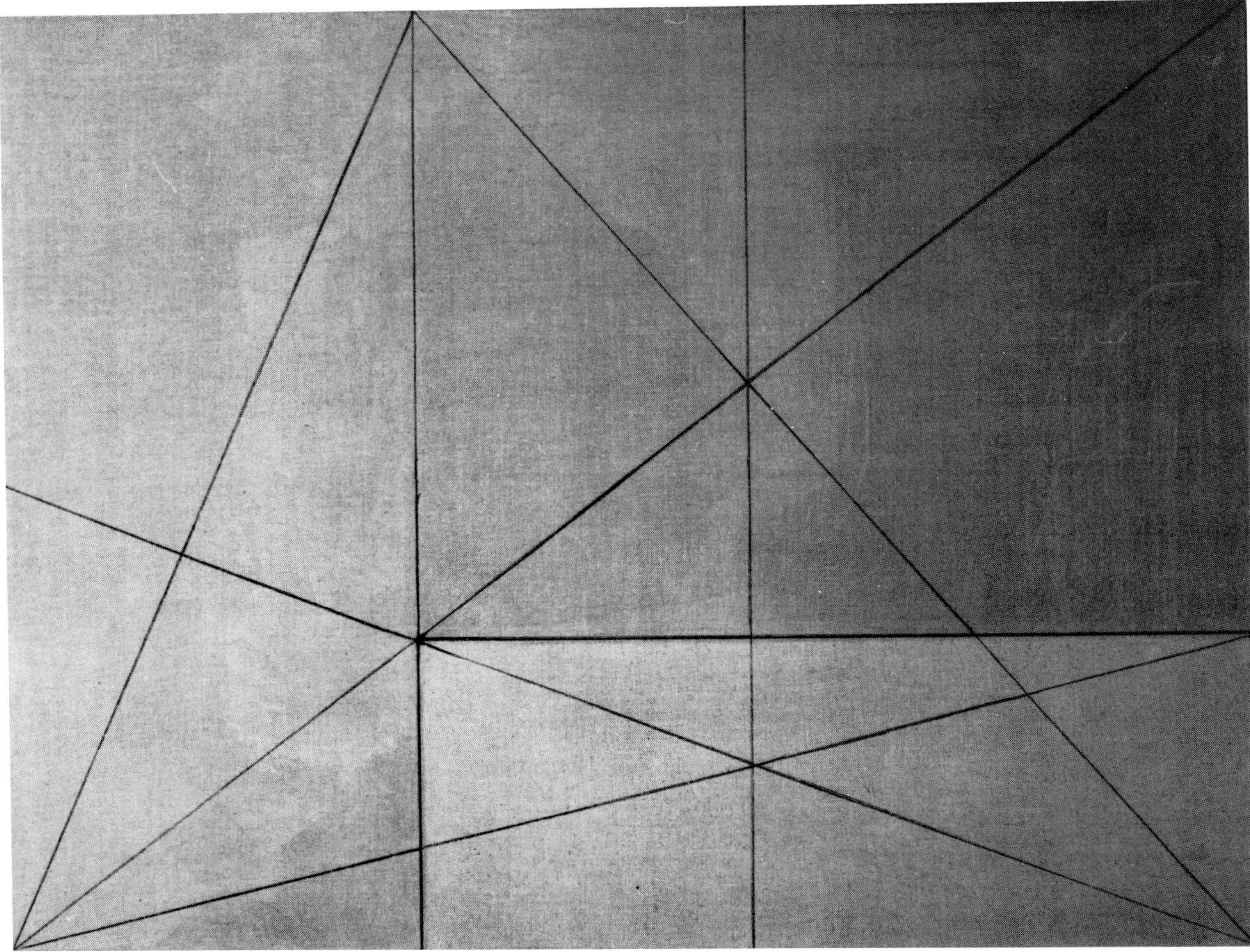

Fig. 2. Underdrawing on canvas, 1981. Three parts: 19½ x
44½", 39 x 15", and 39 x 29½".

Kotik delineates his geometric formats. In fact,
many are based on the Golden Section (fig. 2, ill.
above), an age-old mathematical system of propor-
tions thought to express classical, ideal visual har-
monies. The control and rationality of this
procedure perhaps also derive from Kotik's exten-
sive experience in applied arts and seem to reflect
the sober logic of his at times sophistic treatises and
writings. Kotik's oeuvre also includes a plethora of
loose sketches in which he plays with the color and
the graphic workings in the interior of the predetermined geometric shapes. His gestural charcoal
drawings in particular have great verve and anima-
tion. Such extemporaneous sketches are in themselves highly accomplished works of art and serve,
as well, as preliminary exercises for the act of
painting.

Once Kotik has decided on the geometrics of
his components and has made the canvases, he
works intuitively with the object. Just as the painting process is spontaneous and organic, so may the
object take on assemblage elements or become in-
corporated with drawing on the wall. While work-

ing, Kotik will on very rare occasions endow the
piece with a title (which he generally eschews to
avoid placing an a priori interpretation on the
work). For example, *Quatre figures [Four Fig-
ures]*, 1983, (cat. 29, ill. p. 42), in its unfinished
state evoked for him thoughts of Brancusi's sculpture. Its title, the language of which he carefully
chose, has parallel connotations and implies simultaneously four figures, four forms, four presences
and so on.

The gestural qualities and expressiveness of
Kotik's work have recently reached a new profi-
ciency. His extended stay in New York from 1982
to 1983 had a liberating effect and he has found a
fresh equilibrium between the systemic and the ex-
pressionistic. His use of colors has since become
bolder and his brushwork has achieved a fresh bra-
vura. It is as if he had held the romantic and visionary side of his artistic temperament in careful
check, in order to focus in earnest on abstract conceptual issues.

.   .   .   .

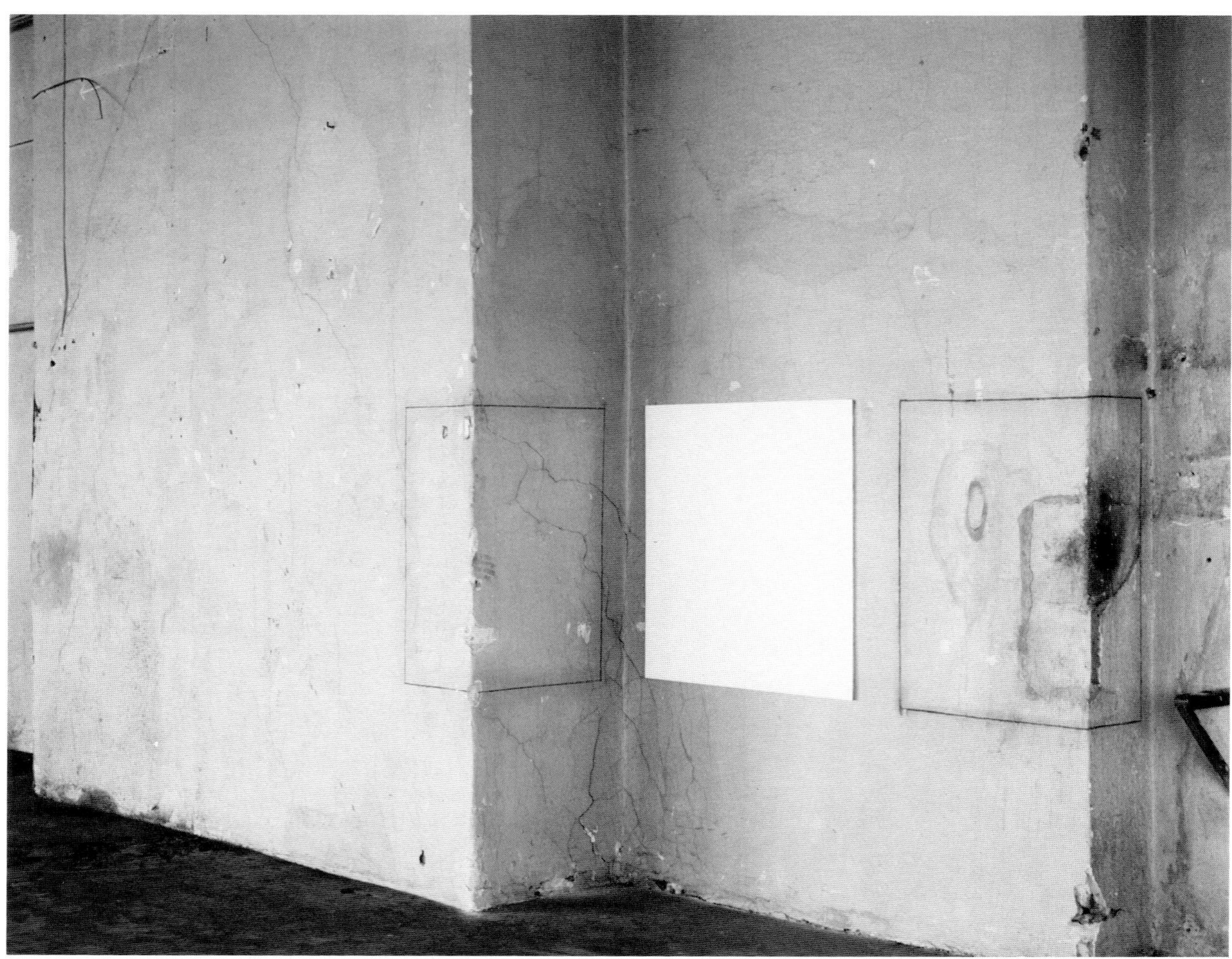

Installation for *Raume,* exhibition at an alternative space on
Lützowstrasse, West Berlin, 1978. Charcoal wall drawing and
paper.

Kotik's evolution as an artist has revolved around the tenet that painting should speak to us through the common dimension of the physical world, yet he feels concurrently that the essence of art resides in its spirituality. True visual understanding comes not by objective observation but through contemplation and slow absorption of a painting. Any work of art, he maintains, functions ultimately in this ritualistic and mythic sphere of experience. In this respect, Kotik's aesthetics reveal strong parallels with the writings of philosopher Ernst Cassirer. In *An Essay on Man*, Cassirer encapsulates the ability of art to transcend profane reality:

> *What we feel in art is not a simple or single emotional quality. It is the dynamic process of life itself —the oscillation between opposite poles, between joy and grief, hope and fear, exultation and despair.*[33]

Cassirer's studies of our perception of reality in anthropological terms further clarify the ways in which Kotik's work addresses us. In his discussion of symbolic forms, Cassirer elucidates the nature of mythical thinking, endemic to all cultures, as that which "seizes upon a very specific and concrete spatial structure in order to carry through its whole 'orientation' of the world."[34] This mythical response is emotional as opposed to cognitive. It is developed largely through our "intuition" of space and form, which is established in part by the experience of contrasts (such as light and dark, up and down, interior and exterior), that impart to every element a unique expressive intonation. Thus our mythical intuition of space, says Cassirer, "occupies a kind of middle position between the space of sense perception and the space of pure cognition, that is geometry."[35] These concepts define precisely the parameters of Kotik's art. The spiritual dynamics in his paintings are sparked by the dialogue between these polarities—the logic of the geometric form and the expressive evocations of the painterly surface.

Similar interest in the mythic and universal of

course underlies most of post-war abstraction. In seeking to create symbolic correspondences for spiritual experience, artists ultimately digressed from observable reality. It would be arduous, if not futile, to attempt to characterize or explain the difference between attitudes of Abstract Expressionism in America and lyrical abstraction in Europe. However, for European artists like Kotik, the immediacy of World War II was, and has remained, a determining factor in their art. The erosion of faith in observable reality and a sense of the random absurdity of the human condition bred intense reactions of existentalism and transcendentalism.

For Kotik, political cataclysm followed closely on the heels of war. Both events robbed him of much desired opportunities and, significantly, contributed to disillusionment and a certain ironic resolve. Art historian Dore Ashton has proposed that irony—which is so apparent in Kotik's attitudes and approach toward art—is one of the qualifying characteristics of contemporary European art, one based on "contradictory modes" of apprehending experience.[36] Whereas the deterministic American artist may believe in absolute discovery, she purports, the European artist focuses on finding and revealing.[37] Her speculation is applicable and instructive in the case of Kotik, who has stated similarly that an artist must "make himself an instrument through which the world resonates."[38] It is important that the formative years of Kotik's artistic thought preceded by decades his opportunity to enact ideas openly and freely: His mature work, which at times may appear deceptively minimalist and formal, has been enriched and tempered by his background of European humanism. As a result, his art has a poignant, metaphorical essence and unique intimacy. In his most recent painterly objects, Kotik has given more breadth to these qualities and has achieved a new maturity of vision that allows him greater expressive latitude. He now shows his full richness as a painter.

Notes

1. Marcel Duchamp, "Statements and Documents: Marcel Duchamp," *Daedalus* (Cambridge: Massachusetts), winter 1960, p. 111. Special issue, "The Visual Arts Today." Reprinted from *ARTnews*, summer 1957.

2. Jiří Kotalík, *Tschechische Kunst des 20. Jahrhunderts: Einige Aspekte der Entwicklung* (Kunsthaus Zürich, Zurich, 1970), pp. 6-8.

3. Dore Ashton, "News from behind the iron curtain," *ARTnews* (New York), vol. 59. No. 7, November 1960, pp. 58, 60.

4. The event was organized by Huelsenbeck, Hausmann and Baeder and appeared in Prague at the Commodities Exchange (March 1) and Mozarteum (March 2). William Rubin, *Dada and Surrealist Art* (New York: Harry N. Abrams, 1969), pp. 458-59.

5. Kramář formed his collection primarily between 1910 and 1913. He had over forty works by Picasso, as well as major paintings by Parisian and Czechoslovakian avant-garde artists. Kramář also published a book, *Kubismus* (Prague, 1921). His collection was bequeathed in 1960 to the National Gallery in Prague (the foundation of which was the Picture Gallery and its collection formed under Kramář's directorship). Jiří Kotalík, "Vincenc Kramář: Homage to an Art Critic," in *Kupka, Gutfreund & C. nella Galleria Nazionale di Praga* (Venice: La Biennale di Venezia, Settore Arti Visive, 1980) pp. 45-46.

6. Other members of *Gruppe 42* (Skupina 42) were artists František Gross, František Hudeček, Kamil Lhoták, Bohumír Matal, Jan Smetana, Karel Souček, and writers Josef Kainar, Jiří Kotalík, Ivan Blatný, Jan Hanč, Jiřina Harková, Jindrich Chalupecký, and artist and poet Jiří Kolář.

7. From author's interview with the artist in West Berlin, July 27, 1983, trans. by David L. Vierling. All other quotes, unless otherwise cited, are from author's conversation with the artist.

8. Ashton, "News from behind the iron curtain," *ARTnews*, p. 31.

9. Jiří Kotalík, *Tschechische Kunst des 20. Jahrhunderts*, p. 16.

10. Anna Balakian, *André Breton: Magus of Surrealism* (New York: Oxford University Press, 1971), p. 159.

11. Interview with the artist by Marina Dinkler and Jes Petersen in the brochure *Jan Kotik: Wandobjekte und Zeichnungen* (West Berlin: Galerie Marina Dinkler and Galerie Petersen, 1983), n.p.

12. Guy Atkins, *Asger Jorn: The crucial years, 1954-1964* (London: Lund Humphries, 1977), pp. 18-20, 51-55. See also John A. Walker, *Glossary of Art, Architecture and Design Since 1945*, 2nd rev. ed. (Hamden, Conn: Linnet Books, 1977), pp. 266-67.

13. In 1957, MIBI allied with the Internationale Situationiste (IS) group, which then published a journal. IS remained active through 1969 and propagated radicalism and the use of graffiti, absurdity, materials of the mass media, etc. Jorn was involved with IS until 1961.

14. See *Il Gesto: Bollettino internazionale d'informazione di Bauhaus Immaginista* (Milan: Editoriale Periodici Italiani), June 1955.

15. See Troels Andersen, "Asger Jorn: The Formative Years," in *Asger Jorn* (New York: The Solomon R. Guggenheim Museum, 1982).

16. Atkins, *Asger Jorn: The Crucial Years, 1954-1964*, pp. 18-20.

17. Ashton, "News from behind the iron curtain," *ARTnews*, p. 60 and Pierre Restany, "Prague: Sisyphe sans Kafka serait Prométhée, *Domus* (Milan), no. 450, May 1967, p. 51.

18. "Aber auch das Tachistische Bild war am Ende wie ein Teig, wie amorphes Protoplasma, das sich ins Uferlose ausgedehnt hat, und das war wiederum, von der anderen Seite her unmen-

schlich, den Absichten des Gottes fremd," [But in the end the *tachiste* picture, too, was like a dough, like amorphous protoplasm, that has extended itself limitlessly, and that on the other hand, seen from the other side, was inhuman, alien to the intentions of the god.], Dinkler and Petersen, *Jan Kotik: Wandobjekte und Zeichnungen*, n.p.

19. Ludmila Vachtová, "Okölo Jana Kotíka," *Výtvarné Umění*, vol. III, no. 18, n.p. Quoted in chronology of *Jan Kotik: Arbeiten 1970-78* (Bochum, West Germany: Museum Bochum, 1978), n.p.

20. "Here where I am," unpublished text, trans. by Dr. Wilma Iggers, 1978, [n.p.].

21. *Il dissenso culturale* (Venice: La Biennale di Venezia, 1977), quoted in chronology of *Jan Kotik: Arbeiten 1970-78*, n.p. Chapter 11 from Lao-tzu quoted from Amos Ih Tiao Chang, *The Existence of Intangible Content in Architectonic Form* (Princeton, New Jersey: Princeton University Press 1956), p. 7. Translations differ greatly. See also *The Way of Lao Tzu*, trans. with comments and notes by Wing-tsit Chan (New York: The Bobbs-Merrill Company, Inc. 1963), p. 119, an adaptation of "The Natural Way of Lao Tzu," in *A Source Book of Chinese Philosophy* (Princeton, New Jersey: Princeton University Press, 1963).

22. "Here where I am," [n.p.]

23. Statement by the artist in the brochure, *Jan Kotik: Komprimationen & recelagen + 2 wandobjekte* (West Berlin: Petersen Galerie, 1981), n.p.

24. Dinkler and Petersen, *Jan Kotik: Wandobjekte und Zeichnungen*, n.p.

25. Excerpt from Chapter 24 of the Lao-tzu (*Tao Te Ching*) in Chan, *The Way of Lao Tzu*, p. 143.

26. Excerpt from Chapter 2 of the Lao-tzu, ibid., p. 101.

27. As, for example, "Act without action. Do without ado. Taste without tasting." Excerpt from Chapter 63 of the Lao-tzu, ibid., p. 212.

28. Artist's statement in brochure *Jan Kotik, Ritualisierung der Zeit* (West Berlin: Amerika Haus/Deutscher Akademischer Austauschdienst (DAAD), 1975.

29. Unpublished statement by the artist, 1975, p. 3.

30. "Here where I am," [n.p.].

31. Ibid.

32. Ibid.

33. Ernst Cassirer, "Art," in *An Essay on Man* (New Haven, Conn: Yale University Press, 1944), 21st printing, 1970, pp. 148-149.

34. Ernst Cassirer, "Mythical Thought," vol. 2 of *The Philosophy of Symbolic Forms* (New Haven, Conn: Yale University Press, 1955), third printing, 1964, p. 93.

35. Ibid., p. 83.

36. See Dore Ashton, *The Unknown Shore: A View of Contemporary Art* (Boston: Little, Brown and Company, 1962), pp. 173-190.

37. Ibid., p. 177.

38. Dinkler and Petersen, *Jan Kotik: Wandobjekte und Zeichnungen*, n.p.

Remarks on the Works of Jan Kotik

Hans-Peter Riese

History as a determining factor

When we speak of the universality of art, we all too often mean the history of European artistic styles in the narrow sense of the word. It was not until this century that we began to understand the universality of art in a political sense, as an intellectual reservoir from which nations and peoples draw strength for survival. A bitterly ironic consequence of the dialectic of history is the fact that suppression and expulsion have contributed significantly to strengthening the unity of artistic expression. Furthermore, this fact has resulted in minimizing national and regional differences. As a result, there has been a fertile interaction between European and American art. It would, however, amount to profound intellectual dishonesty if we were to close our eyes to the dangers of the universality of art. We have no qualms about accepting the contributions of the Russian avant-garde in the first twenty years of this eventful century; yet in this instance, aesthetic judgment is separated from the specific historical framework in which the art was created. The formal standards on which we base our judgments have freed themselves from the historical context in which the works were made. We have become insensitive to the way in which artistic development is dependent on historical processes. This has the culminating effect that art is always struggling for survival against historical and political trends.

To examine the work of an artist like Jan Kotik from the viewpoint of how it might have developed under different political conditions would be nothing more than a fruitless intellectual game. It is necessary to evaluate his work within the context in which it was created in order to see the core of Kotik's motivation.

Jan Kotik was born in Turnov, Czechoslovakia in 1916, and has suffered the history of his people as a human being and as a political individual. The years of his youth and university studies were a period of national liberation, and, from 1918 onward, renewal of national and cultural identity. Kotik also experienced the ensuing period of fascist occupation and suppression. His search for artistic identity took place in an atmosphere of deprivation, in resistance to the strident doctrines of the National Socialists.[1] For Jan Kotik, the awareness that art has to struggle against political circumstances was to be a primary factor throughout his lifetime.

The fact that an individualistic and independent intellectual like Kotik joined a coalition of artists in 1942, when he was 26, was based upon a belief that an individual in isolation is unable to act against the political trends of the times. What is required instead is the collective solidarity of those who pursue common objectives, yet do not want to be restricted in their creative individuality. On a purely political level, this belief induced Kotik to join the Resistance against the National Socialist occupiers, a fact for which he was decorated after the war.

The stylistic characteristics of the works of the various members of *Gruppe 42* are of interest. These artists manifested an intellectual interest in their surroundings. They studied the emotional world of modern man and the problems of living in a technological, urban landscape. Although technological advance and modernization were products of the then dominant ideology, these artists were beginning to realize that such a notion of progress could potentially become an instrument of suppression. Along with this awareness came an understanding that active contact with artistic developments outside the ideological and political realm was a necessity for survival. Years later, after National Socialist ideology was replaced by communist ideology, Kotik contradicted Socialist Realism with the insight, "…that a work of art must be able to influence the entire formative (material) culture…."[2] The interesting thing about this remark, made in 1950, is the fact that Kotik began systematically to expand the concept of the unity of the visual arts. Areas of design, and particularly the planning of one's environment, were subject to an aesthetic ideal which in itself represented grounds for resistance to the prevailing political and ideological restrictions. These existential values in contemporary art affected the individual's relationship to the art movement, and hence the concept of universality took on a new meaning.

Kotik has long been conscious of the meaning of his artistic life, an awareness that became a necessity in the historical circumstances under which he was forced to live and work. The major international influences in art at that time, post-Cubism and post-Surrealism, had to be defended against the ideological claims of National Socialism. After the war, bits and pieces of information on the art of the 1950s (*informel*) and the 1960s (object art) trickled into the country. This was a programmatic resistance to the domination of doctrinaire Socialist Realism. It was above all this critical interest in art movements outside of his own country that en-

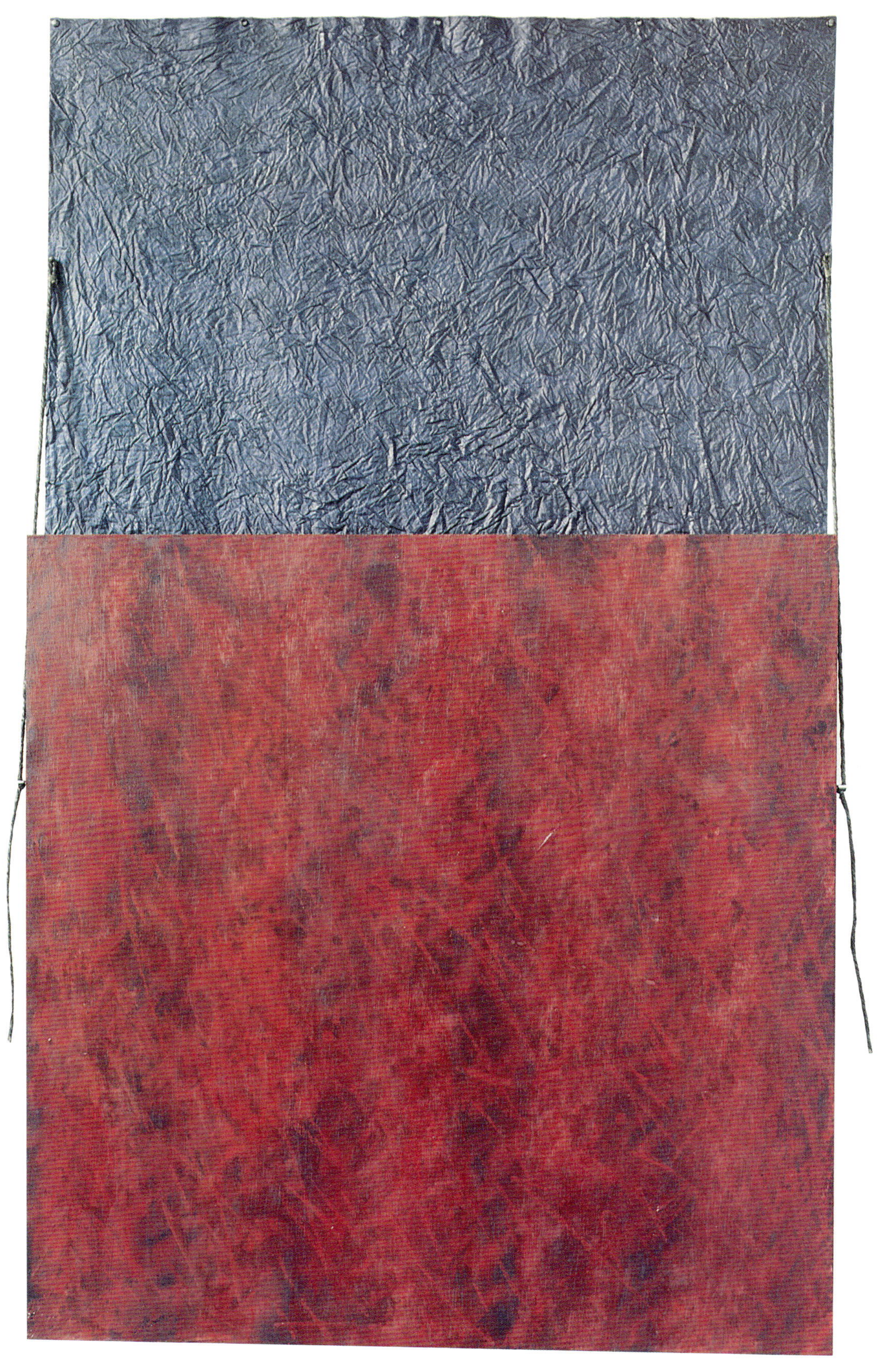

8. *Untitled*, 1977
    acrylic on canvas, string
    48½ × 29⅛″

abled Kotik to preserve a unique artistic identity. His work is characterized by an autonomous approach and continuity, capable of embracing the universality of art in political terms, and yet of providing a means of securing itself against ideological claims.

Continuity and autonomy

Jan Kotik speaks of the necessity of destroying previous artistic orders to arrive at an individual pictorial language. This he sees as a liberation from the traditional posture of defense and mere conservation. Kotik and other *Gruppe 42* artists recognized very quickly that their individual styles were too closely related to the examples of art they wanted to defend and preserve for the benefit of general culture. Liberation could only take place through the relationship between the artist and his aesthetic product. Ludmila Vachtová, the most intelligent and sensitive historian of contemporary Czech art, describes this process in Kotik:

> *His development at that time casts a somewhat different light on all those basically romantic theories on alienation, existential fears and burning one's way through the layers of the essential core of the person, i.e. the theory of the mechanical transference of the external atmosphere into the reality of the picture of the theory of art as a contemporary document. Kotik lived just as intensively as all the others, perhaps even more so thanks to his political insights. However, the harsher the situations were, the more intimate his pictures became. Sometimes they even reflected a measure of well-being, not in the sense of genre painting, but rather in the overall structuring of the picture. The painter was struggling to survive. However, he succeeded in freeing his work of signs of this struggle. It reflected his striving for freedom....*[3]

This development took place from 1950 to 1960, a particularly oppressive period in terms of cultural policy.

From the outset, the formal basis of Kotik's work lay more in the traditions of Cubism and post-Surrealism, both of which tended to give strong emphasis to formal and graphic elements. The pictorial structure in his work was subjected to a conscious and controlled destruction. The graphic emphasis of lines, the use of black and the autonomous structuring of the surface of the picture all played an important role. An inner tension is manifested in the pictures Jan Kotik painted in the first half of the 1950s. This tension, a conflict between the "lyrical" and the "dramatic," was to remain a permanent source of innovation. Works from this period manifest a primary concern for the stylistic element. Color is used in moderation, as a balancing factor. (This was to change, particularly as a result of Kotik's acquaintance with the paintings of the Cobra group and with Asger Jorn. Color then became the vehicle of dramatic expressiveness.) In the isolation of his studio, Kotik went through all the developmental phases that were to parallel contemporary art movements in the West.

In spite of this isolation, Kotik found that he was able to pursue his artistic interests in the public sphere of industrial design; this provided him with an opportunity to test his own ideals on the unity of artistic thought and was also a source of feedback for his development.

From 1947 to 1950 Kotik worked as the head of the industrial design atelier at the Center for Applied Arts in Prague with Vanek, an architect who had studied under Adolf Loos.[4] The stringency of the formal structures throughout Kotik's oeuvre doubtlessly derives ultimately from the theory of aesthetic functionality that he developed as a designer and elaborated in numerous theoretical writings.

Kotik had for the first time the opportunity to present his works to a broader public in 1957. The retrospective had a shock effect and sparked a cultural policy debate. There is no common denominator for Kotik's efforts to find his own pictorial style in this crucial year; however, the kernels of later developments are clearly visible. Most noticeable is the complete absence of pictorialism and instead the creation of "imaginative images" (Vachtová) developed in the process of painting and legitimized on the basis of the laws of their inner structure. Kotik's constant critical alertness is reflected when he says:

> *When we lay down our brush to see what has been completed at a given moment, how far we have come, it is all the better if an experienced critic dwells within us as well.*

It is this rare combination of talent and the ability to monitor his own work that enabled Kotik to achieve autonomy in his art during these years. When Kotik attended a congress entitled "*Mouvement international pour un Bauhaus imaginiste,*" organized by Asger Jorn in Alba, Italy in 1956, the result was a sudden and fruitful relationship with movements that had originated in an unrestricted environment. For the first time, Kotik was encouraged by the other painters in attendance and saw his own art confirmed in their work.

The congress confirmed two dominant elements of his development at the time: the dissolution of graphic pictorial structure into free gesture, and the eradication of the two-dimensional surface by means of spacial extension. That Kotik was not influenced by external sources is proven by a note he wrote dating from 1942:

> An object, eliminating the flat surface picture, would be a rigorous solution. It ought to stand out from the wall.

This crucial development in Kotik's work was motivated by his internal evolution and by the exceptionally large role intellectual reflection plays for him. We should not lose sight of these factors — they are pivotal components in Kotik's work. Kotik is the opposite of a spontaneous artist in the French sense of an *écriture mécanique*. In this way, he differs considerably from a number of *informel* artists of the 1950s. The theoretical reflection that always accompanied and controlled his artistic process enabled him to work out formal structures, and the connections that formed, as it were, a system of aesthetic coordinates. In "Remarks on Intelligibility — The Meaning of the Work of Art" Kotik writes:

> *The entire production of artistic works forms a multi-dimensional structure extended in space, time, traditions (both artistic and intellectual), and varying abilities to be "contemporary." It is limited to the direct and indirect influence of people. Its structural elements, which influence each other reciprocally (influence of one group of artists on another, one period on another), are influenced (by art consumers, by the environment we live in and ideas from other spheres of life) and exert influence (on art consumers and on other fields of creative activity).*

In these reflections, Kotik developed the concepts central to his art — space and time. These coordinates of human life secure the inner continuity and autonomy of Kotik's works in a manner that emphasizes the relationship between art and the world, and between art and its beholder.

Process and ritual

His works prior to 1957, the year of his major exhibition at the Writers Union in Prague,[5] make it clear that Kotik, like other artists, had taken a course that led to the formulation of his own semiotic alphabet. The crucial factor in this development was the painter's need to separate himself from the prefabricated idea of a picture. The picture no longer appeared as an end in itself. Instead, it manifested itself as an ongoing process, which formulated an artistic syntax in its course. On this subject Kotik has written:

> *A good* tachiste *picture does not presuppose the idea, the concept of the finished picture, but rather the selection of a specific method for its realization, a physical method.*

The results of these early insights were much more determined by a liberation of forms than by the artist's devotion to the method of creation. The pictures painted during these years show a certain stylistic variation. They are reminiscent, in part, of the beginnings of modern art. Kotik has an exact knowledge of art history and points to similar lines of development in the painters of the Blaue Reiter group, particularly Kandinsky. But Kotik's art, and that of a number of his friends and colleagues, was still in the process of freeing itself from its defensive posture.

When Kotik, like his contemporaries Jorn, Dubuffet, Vedova, Fautrier, Saura or van de Velde, turned away from further development of the traditional pictorial idea, and turned to the study of the artistic material itself, he encountered problems that required a different solution. The means used to create a painting were suddenly unsuitable for the creation of paintings not derived from nature but rather parallel to it. This new orientation affected the "physical" method of painting, as well as the material employed. In this sense, the materiality of paint was explored. The canvas, too, acquired a new status that freed it from the sole function of bearing a pictorial illusion. This changed the relationship of the painter to his medium. In an unprecedented manner, the physical vitality of the artist was drawn into the painting process.

It was not surprising that both the artists of the *informel* group developing in the West and Kotik shortly arrived at a critical threshold. Differentiation in their methods had led to a breakdown of aesthetic unity, referred to as the crisis of *tachisme. Tachiste* forays into new artistic terrain had promoted formulation of uniform semiotic or iconic languages. Kotik, isolated as he was, was nonetheless apparently aware of this danger early on and consequently did not succumb to it. Despite his liberation through the painterly gesture and the resultant confrontation with materials, by the end of the 1950s Kotik had become interested primarily in the role of "process" in the creation of paintings. He realized that it would be impossible

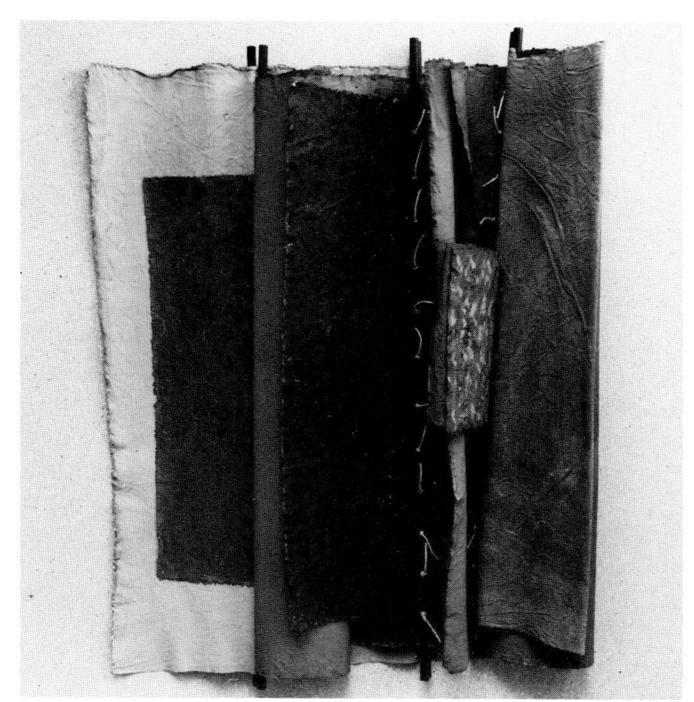

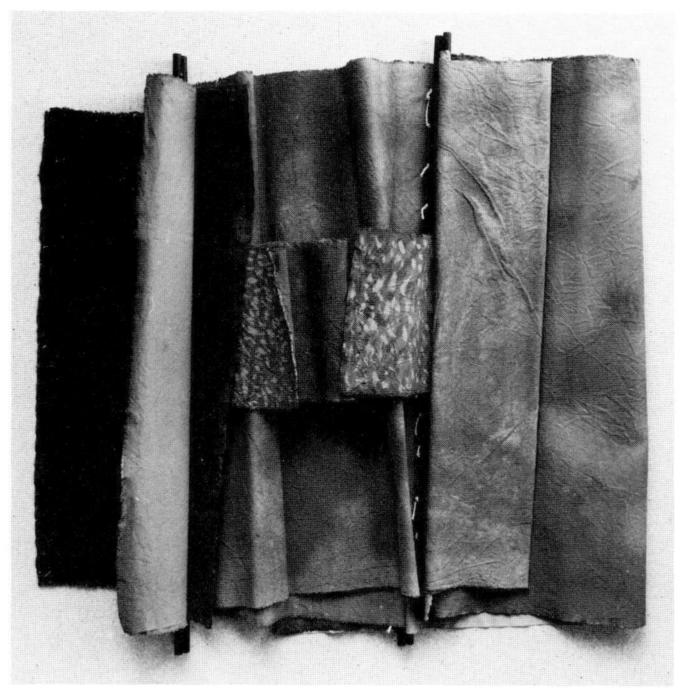

1. *Object transformable*
[Transformable object], 1972-73
acrylic on canvas, wood
dimensions variable
(fabric: 26 × 35″)

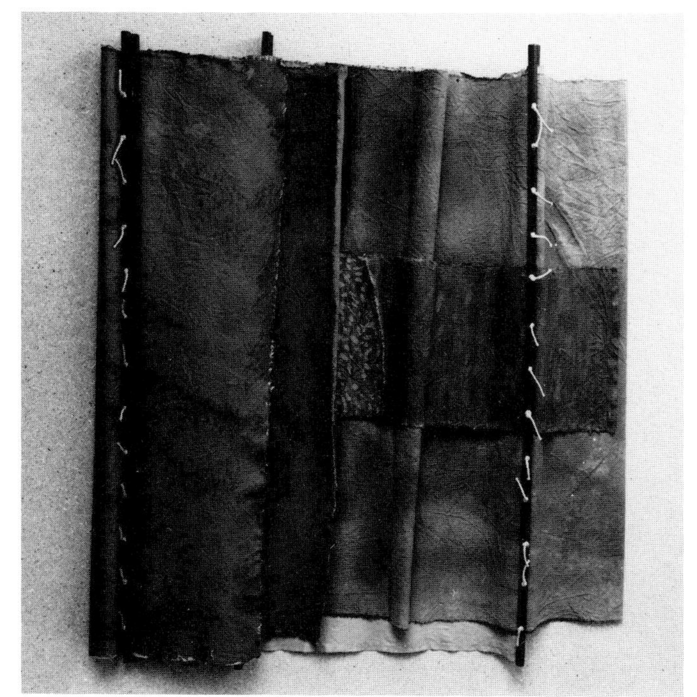

to break through the barrier of the two-dimensionality of the surface if the illusionist components of *tachisme* were not overcome. Thus, he astutely determined the problem that eventually led to the break-up of *tachisme* as a stylistic movement, and subsequently concentrated on issues of space and time.

He analyzed these dual aspects separately in this developmental phase. The spatial question had bothered Kotik ten years earlier and the note he wrote in 1952 proves that he was already interested in breaking out of the strictures imposed by a two-dimensional surface. Kotik knew that the space in front of and behind the surface could only be used if illusionism were eliminated. He also knew this was possible at several levels. It was possible to "stage" paintings as "real space" by taking the canvases off the wall, and structuring them to form a space that could be walked through. It was also possible to concentrate on the constituent materials. Carried to its logical conclusion, this would lead to sculpture, to the occupation of space by material. Although Kotik is often strongly object-oriented, he at no time crossed the dividing line between painting and sculpture. For him sculpture, like the return of *tachiste* painting to figuration, would be too conventional and retrogressive.

In an article written in 1966, Kotik made a statement about the two-dimensional surface that marked the beginning of his development of the third dimension:

> *If we stick with the picture (as an object) and the surface, since it represents a real (non-illusionist) element, then the question arises as to what takes place on this surface, aside from the fact that it exists, and what movement takes place on it.*

The movement on the canvas, depicted in the structure of the pictorial gesture, is just as real as the canvas itself. The course of movement depicted in the given structure is the time of the painter's gesture. It is, as it were, the time invested by the painter which appears "frozen" in the picture. In *informel* painting this concept of time confronted the time of the viewer—the time of perception. In essence the viewer was now called upon to reenact the "invested time" of the creator, to participate actively in decoding the pictorial structure of the painting and to experience it as real time. In this sense, the dimension known as "production time," as an element separately bound up with the structure of the picture and its material existence, falls together with the real time involved in "reading" the picture. There is no longer a fictitious time dimension as in classical illusionis-

tic pictures of the modern era. Instead there is only real time.

There is a further barrier when speaking of a picture as a thing bounded by a two-dimensional surface observed at a specific time—the phenomenon of the third dimension. The modern era has seen a number of different ways of introducing the third dimension. Arsén Pohribný pointed out that Kotik:

> *…reproduces time and real space by means of systems of signs that are verified and, at the same time, become experienced on the basis of our actions.*[6]

This emphasizes that Kotik was not interested exclusively in pictorial problems. Instead he refers to the metaphysical meanings that bring his works into contact with the universals of human existence. As Pohribný put it:

> *Kotik's pictorial instruments become a connecting element between the subjective microcosm and the universe.*[7]

Kotik's art never crosses over into the area of pure philosophical reflection such as is the case with some Conceptual artists. In analyzing Kotik's works, we are constantly confronted with their material appearance, i.e. their real existence as a prerequisite for their metaphysical identity. This dimension of materiality is determined by Kotik's use of paint and canvas.

Over the course of the decade, Kotik's personal circumstances changed dramatically. In the mid-sixties, acquaintance and interaction with artistic developments elsewhere were established. The elements "isolation", "lack of information" and "political pressure" were gone. Kotik's works from the 1960s and 1970s cannot necessarily be subjected to the same analysis. Although Kotik took virtually the same direction as many other painters in the 1960s, his points of departure were entirely different as a result of his particular circumstances.

In the late sixties and early seventies, Kotik continued to experiment with spatial concepts. The canvas was removed from the frame and existed on its own as "cloth." A combination of canvas and paint was then produced as an inseparable unit. Kotik discovered that the harmonious union of paint and canvas eliminated the conflict between "surface" and "paint." He noted that something new had been created with a life of its own. He produced paint-soaked canvases that hung on the wall like stiff cloths or lay on the floor. Fixing the painting to a frame had produced the problem of "surface" and placed the viewer in a position of

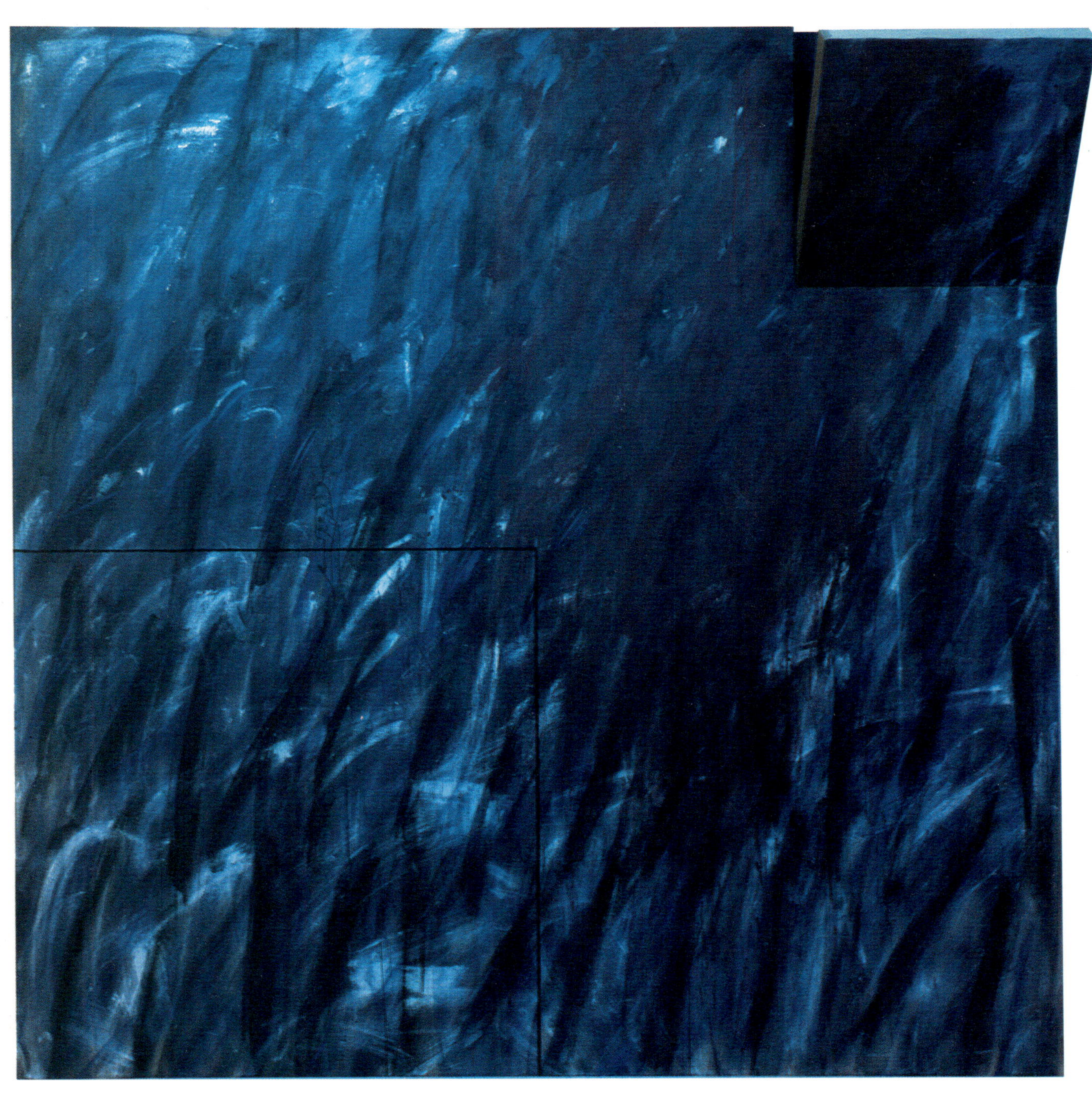

11. *Untitled* , 1980
    tempera and wax on canvas
    two parts:
    78¾ × 78¾″
    19½ × 19½″

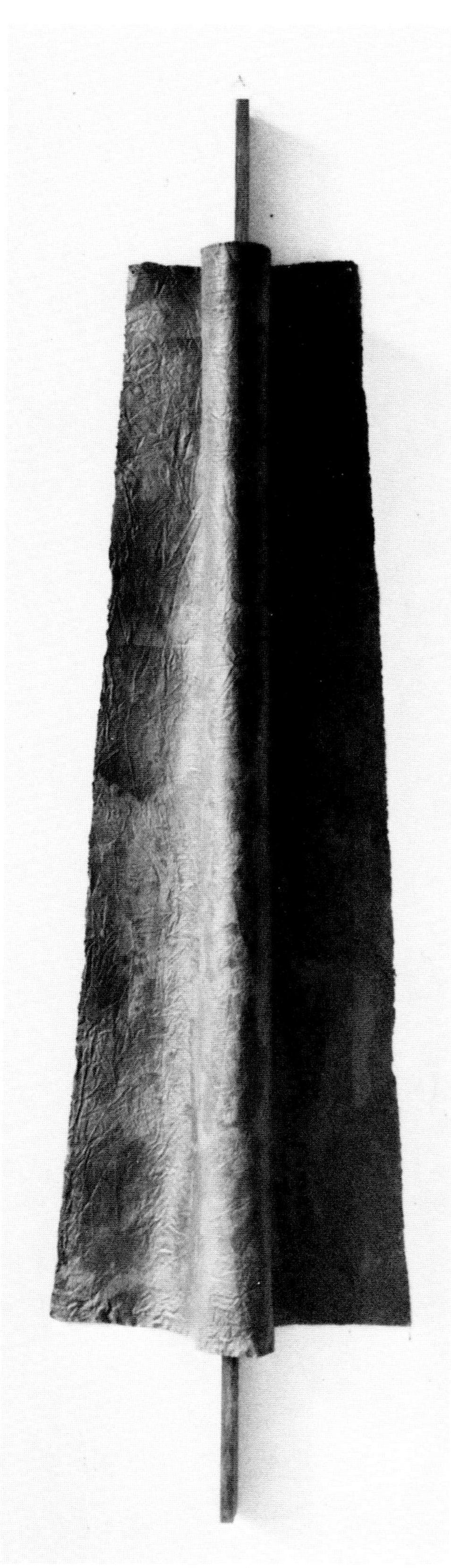

3. *Untitled*, 1975-76
acrylic on canvas, wood
56 × 13"

passivity. By removing the painting from the frame and the wall and making it an object, Kotik granted the viewer an active role. The work could now be modified and recreated variously with the intervention of the viewer.

This development resulted in a visualization of time. After the beholder was ascribed an active role, time was no longer understood as a parallel experience based on the act of decoding. In this phase Kotik encountered a new problem in that the meaning of his objects had to be embodied in the structure of the objects themselves. Kotik at this point could have removed his art from the specific sphere of the artistic and extended it into that of life. In doing so he would have joined the artistic sector that promotes the theory—just as tenacious as it is wrong—that art is life and life is art. Instead, he saw the necessity of reflecting on the mythological value of art. Kotik feels that traditional cultural myths were irretrievably lost more than 150 years ago, and that the remaining relics inhibit the way people approach art. Thus, Kotik structured his objects in such a way that only a predetermined, "ritualized" approach was possible. His works then entered a magical sphere from which art had been expelled. Kotik was aware of the fact that:

> *there are no ready-made rituals at the present time, since their basis, the great mythologies, died out.*

What kind of meditative rituals does Kotik demand of his viewers? They are in actuality premythological rituals, ones that derive from immediate human needs. For Kotik, this is expressed by a kinetic involvement with the work which contributes to the physical process of its creation. With this, Kotik returned to a hope held dear by the avant-garde of the twentieth century, that an integration art and life might be restored. He felt they should be restored through a dialectical relationship between the viewer and the object.

Kotik opened his works of art to life by allowing them to be modified by the viewer. The work transcended its material existence via its ritualistic aspects. Its meaning is not fixed, but is contained as a *potential* that is freed by the actions and reflections of the beholder. He has explained:

> *Just as a jug is made for water that will flow into it, we can design objects today that contain the proposition for certain actions. All that remains is belief; if things exist here with their ritual functionality, tomorrow they will be able to influence the ritualization of forms and make living together possible.*

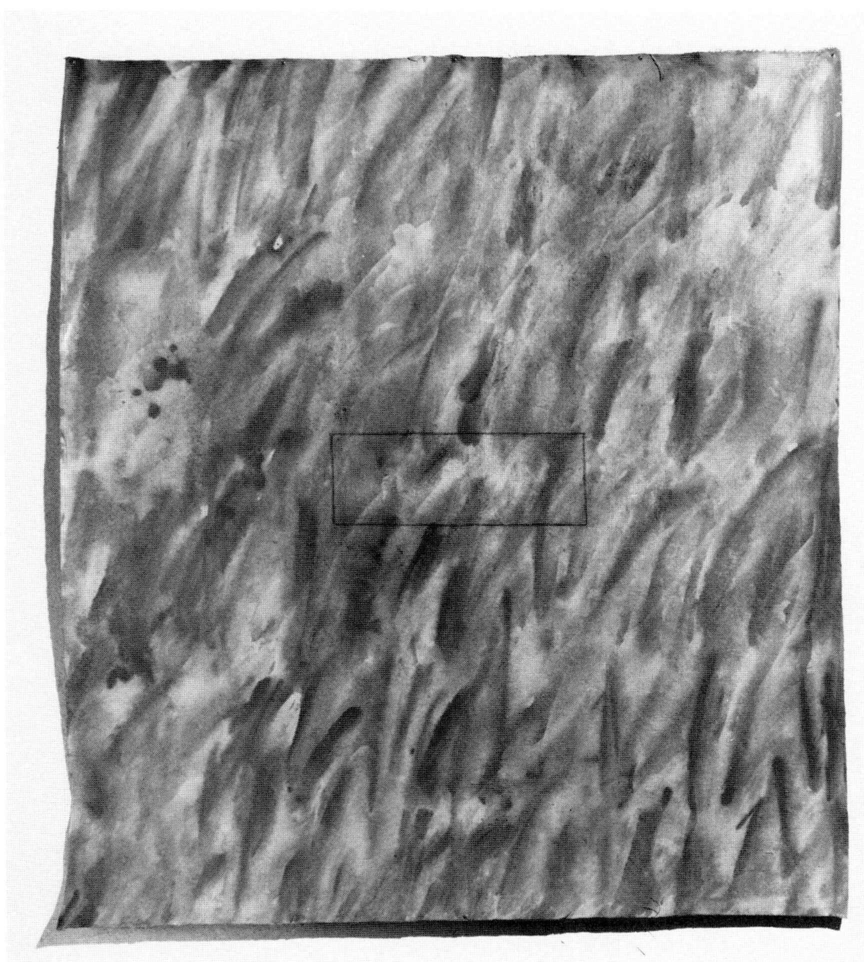

4. *Untitled*, 1976-77
   acrylic on canvas,
   57½ × 52½″

6. *Untitled*, 1976-77
   acrylic on canvas, string
   27 × 37″

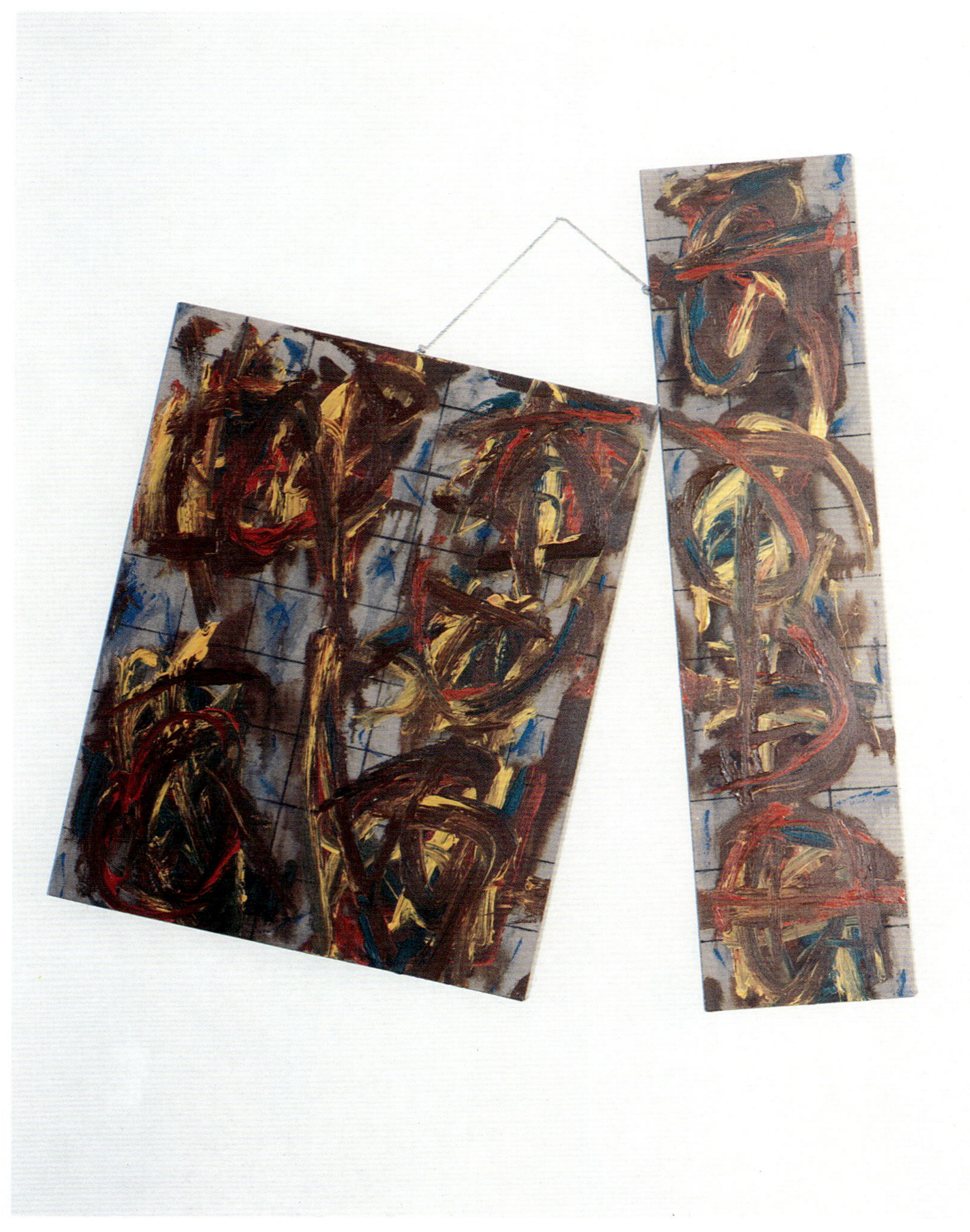

21. *Untitled*, 1982
    acrylic on canvas, rope
    two parts:
    51 × 42"
    72 × 18"

Painting as an ideal

It is characteristic of Kotik that he did not stop exploring at this stage of his development. Painting has continued taking him back, pendulum-like, to phases in which he attempted to re-acquire his artistic instruments. Recent works document what might be called a return to the pictorial gesture, to pure painting. However, it would be misleading if we did not take into consideration the fact that these pictures manifest the experience he has accumulated over the past twenty years. The fact that Kotik has returned to the use of the painterly gesture of the 1960s, or at least appears to be doing so, means that he has resumed a developmental line that had to be broken off because it previously bore no fresh solutions. What finally distinguishes Kotik's most recent works is their skilled combination of pictorial gesture and formal stringency. In the 1950s, the development of these two lines diverged. The combination of the two could have forced Kotik, as it did Mathieu, to develop a system of signs that would have led to a rigidity in his painting. On the other hand, the complete autonomy of pictorial gesture was never a subject of discussion with Kotik, since that would have contradicted his ideas on form. Today the painterly gesture has become a means of artistic expression for him. This is neither related to current trends such as "Wild Painting" or the "New Fauves," nor is it a regression. It is instead an evolutionary process by which the painter tests his artistic potential.

The beholder, once invited to assume an active role, is now forced to a certain distance from the work of art. The focus is now on the identification of the artist by means of the painting he has produced. In these new paintings, Kotik has regained the authoritative presence he had consciously given up. Anyone who is willing to try to understand the recent works of Jan Kotik within this context will see them as the return of a painter to himself, a return that is not to be understood as a 180° turnabout, but rather as the sum of his experience to date.

Hans-Peter Riese writes art criticism for the newspapers Die Zeit *and* Frankfurter Allgemeine Zeitung Für Deutschland. *He was a correspondent in Prague from 1970-1973. Mr. Riese lives in Bonn.*

Notes

1. The Nationalist Socialist German Workers' Party is the official title of the Nazi Party.

2. All statements by Jan Kotik are excerpted from selected writings by the artist cited in the catalogue *Jan Kotik: Arbeiten 1970-78* (Bochum: West Germany: Museum Bochum, 1978). Translations are by the author.

3. Ludmila Vachtová, "Okölo Jana Kotika," *Výtvarné Umění*, vol. III, no. 18, n.p. Quoted in chronology of *Jan Kotik: Arbeiten 1970-78* (Bochum: West Germany: Museum Bochum, 1978), n.p.

4. Adolf Loos (1870-1933), a native of Brno, Czechoslovakia, was a pioneer in the modern architectural movement in Europe.

5. Galerie Topíč

6. Asén Pohribný, "Vom Bild zum Gemälde als 'Realfaktor" in Jan *Kotik: Arbeiten 1970-78* (Bochum, West Germany: Museum Bochum, 1978), n.p.

7. Ibid.

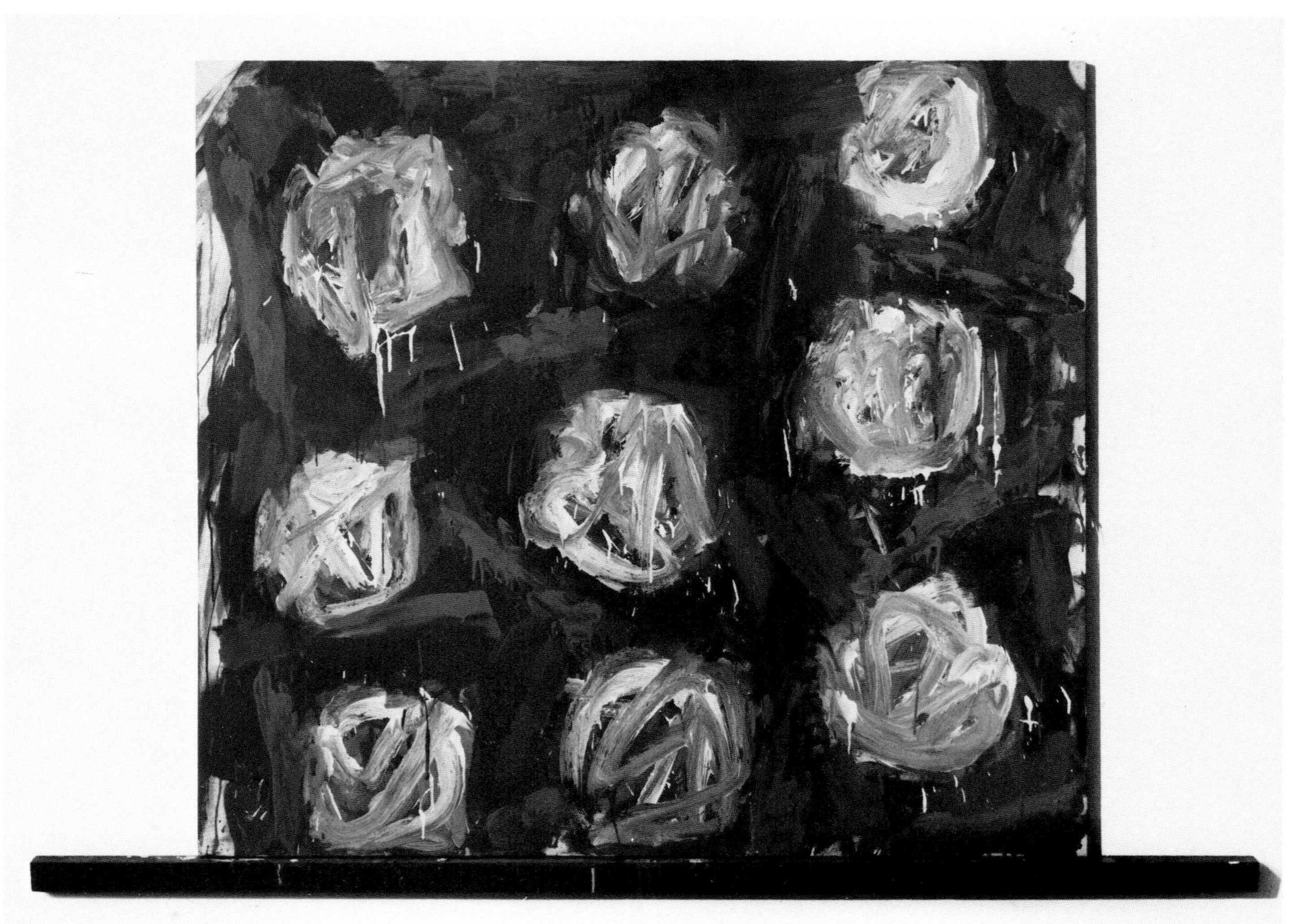

12. *Untitled*, 1980
    acrylic on canvas, wood
    two parts:
    57 × 51″
    2 × 79 × ½″

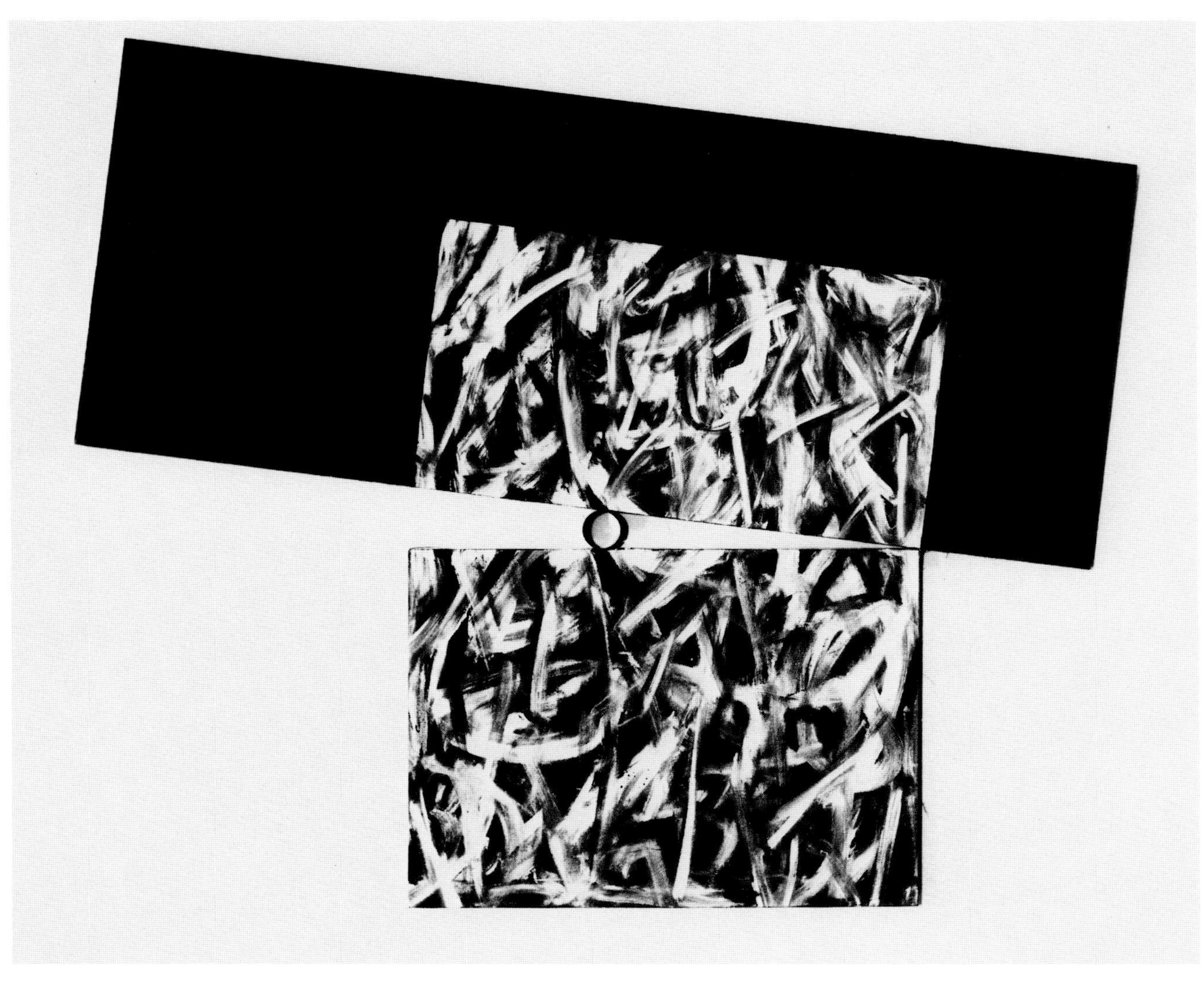

13. *Untitled*, 1980
    acrylic and aluminum on canvas, plastic
    two parts:
    31½ × 78¾"
    27½ × 39⅜"

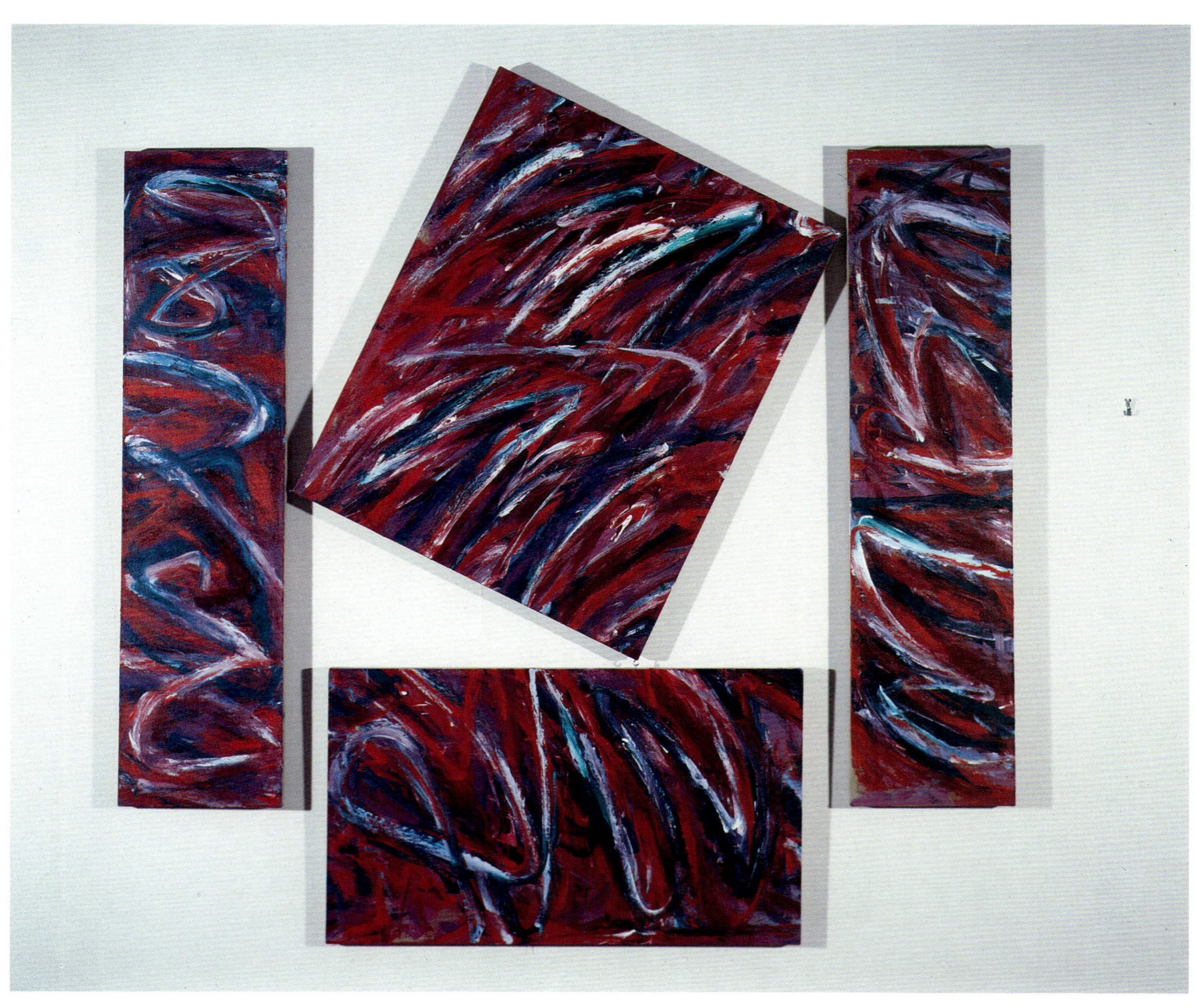

25. *Untitled*, 1982-83
    acrylic on canvas
    four parts:
    two, 72 × 18″ each
    42 × 52″
    30 × 52″

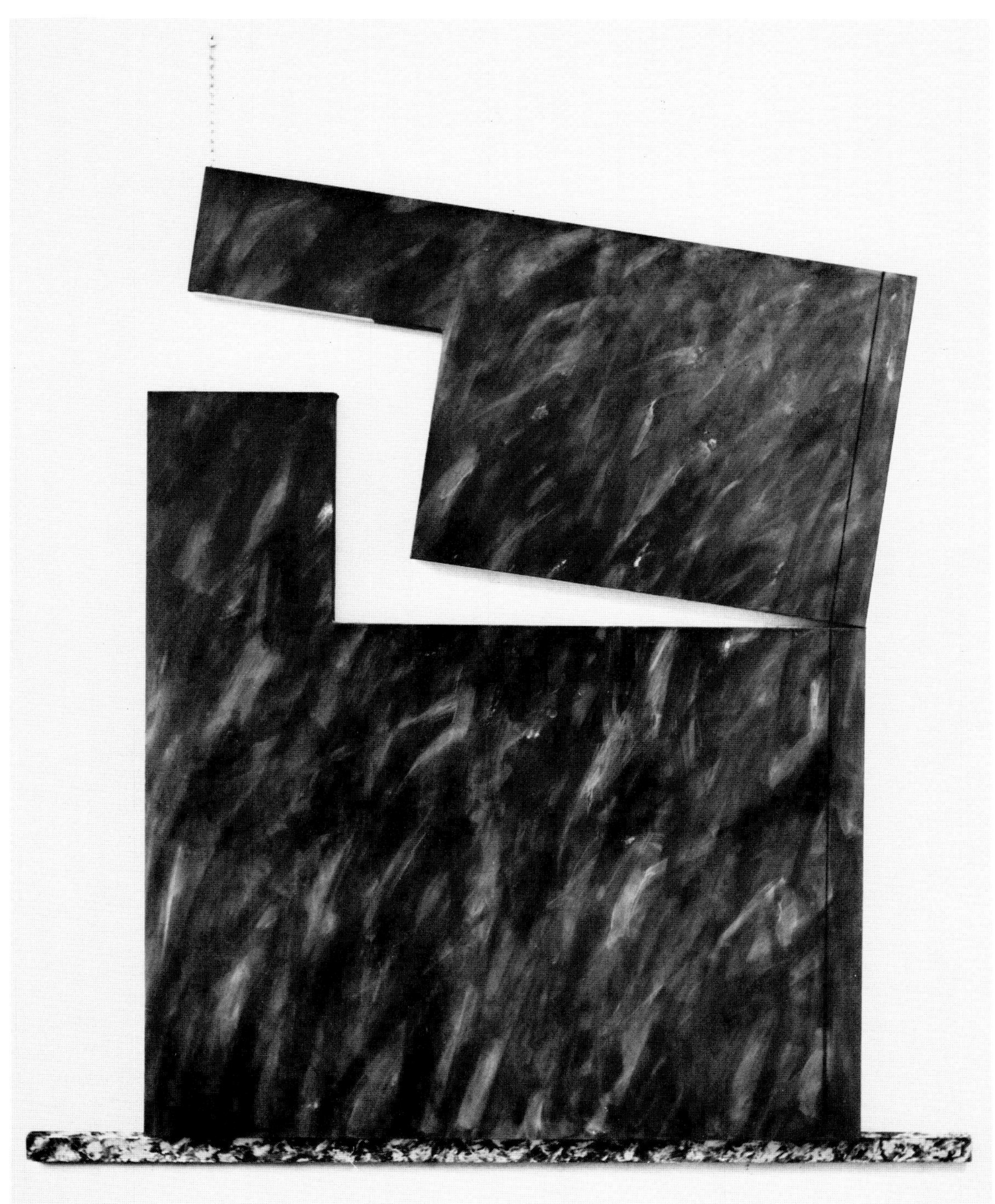

15. *Untitled*, 1980
wax, tempera and charcoal on canvas, acrylic,
graphite and aluminum on wood, chain
three parts:
29⅛ × 59⅛″
61⅛ × 59⅛″
2 × 78¾ × 1½″

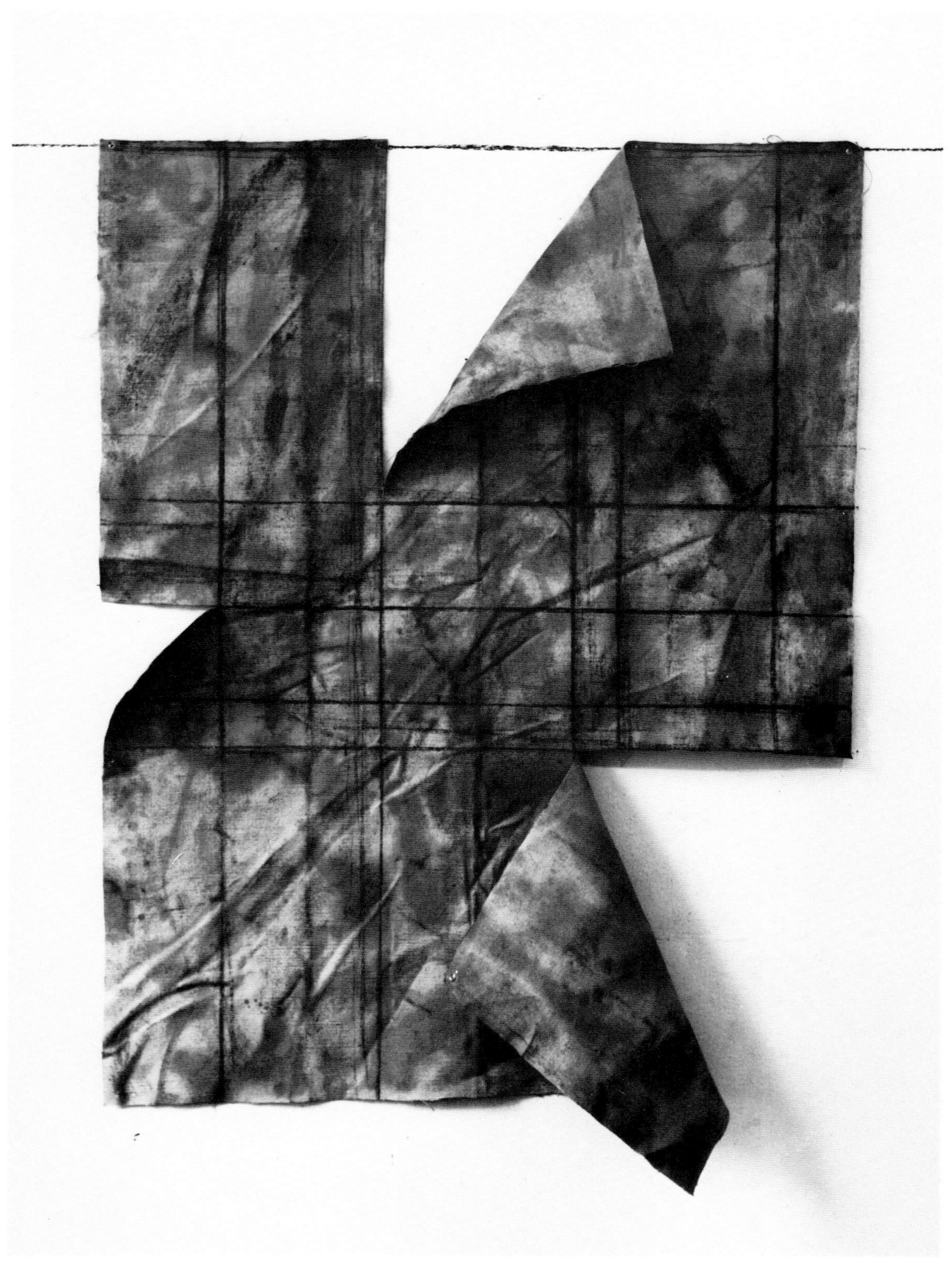

18. *Untitled*, 1981
charcoal and stain on canvas
49 × 38¼″

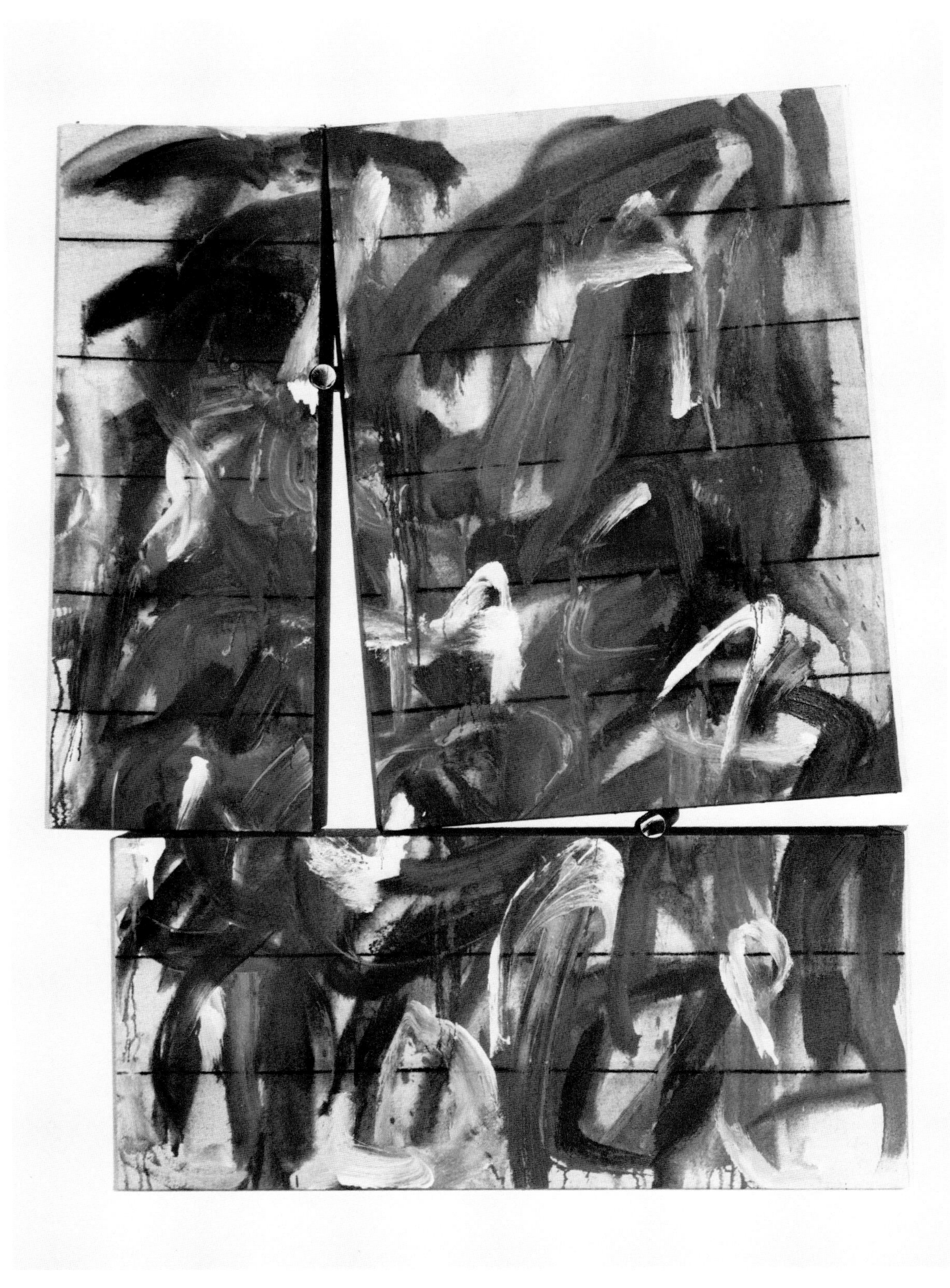

19. *Untitled*, 1981
   acrylic and charcoal on canvas, wood
   three parts:
   19½ × 44½"
   39 × 15"
   39 × 29¼"

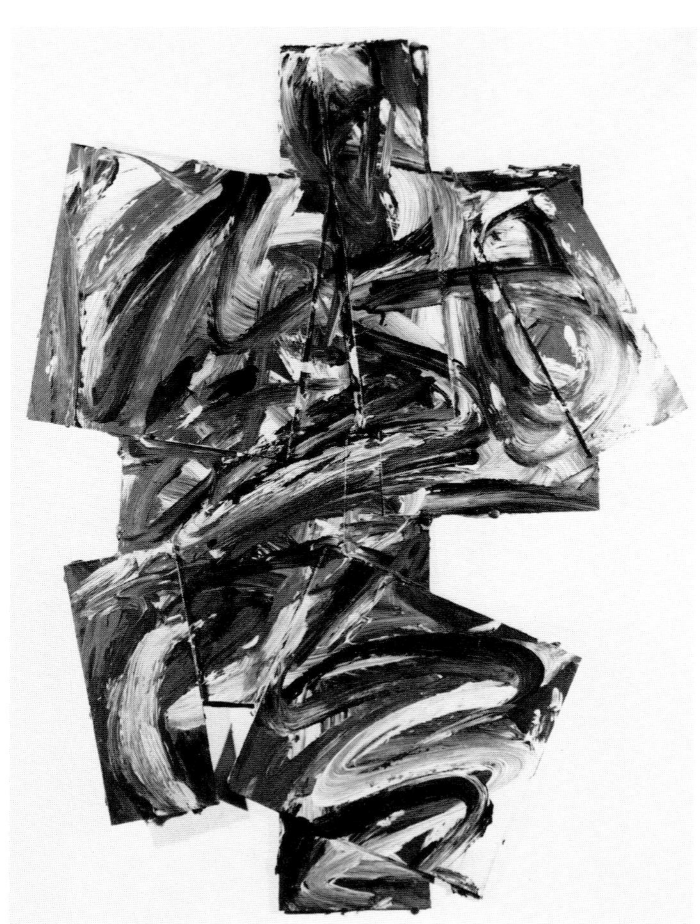

22. *Untitled*, 1982
   acrylic on paper board
   30½ × 30″
   Collection Steven and Cecile Biltekoff, Buffalo

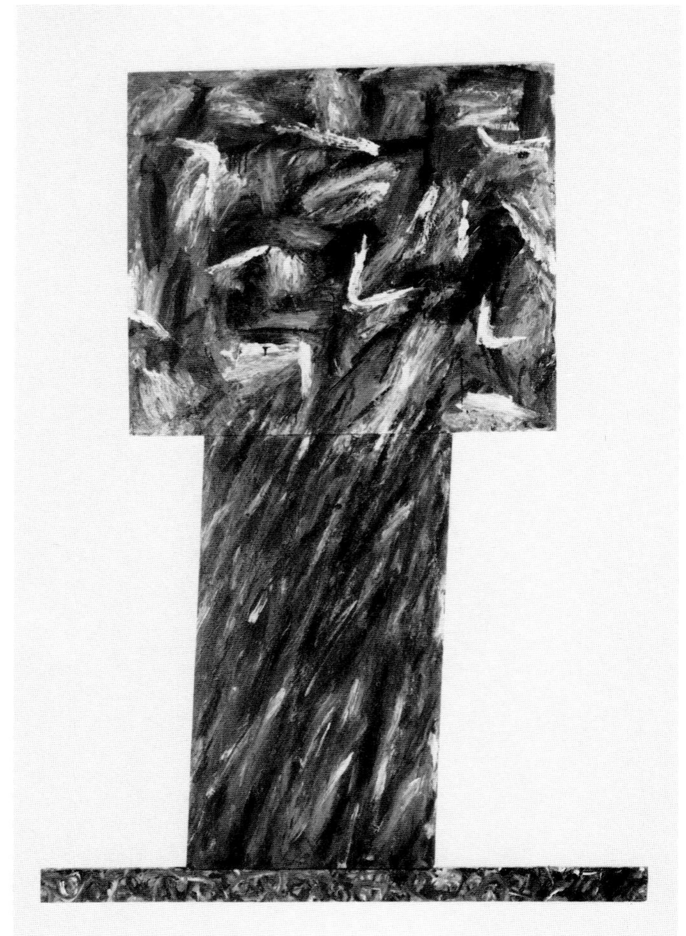

20. *Untitled*, 1982
   acrylic on canvas, wood
   three parts:
   42 × 52″
   72 × 18″
   4 × 73⅝ × 2″

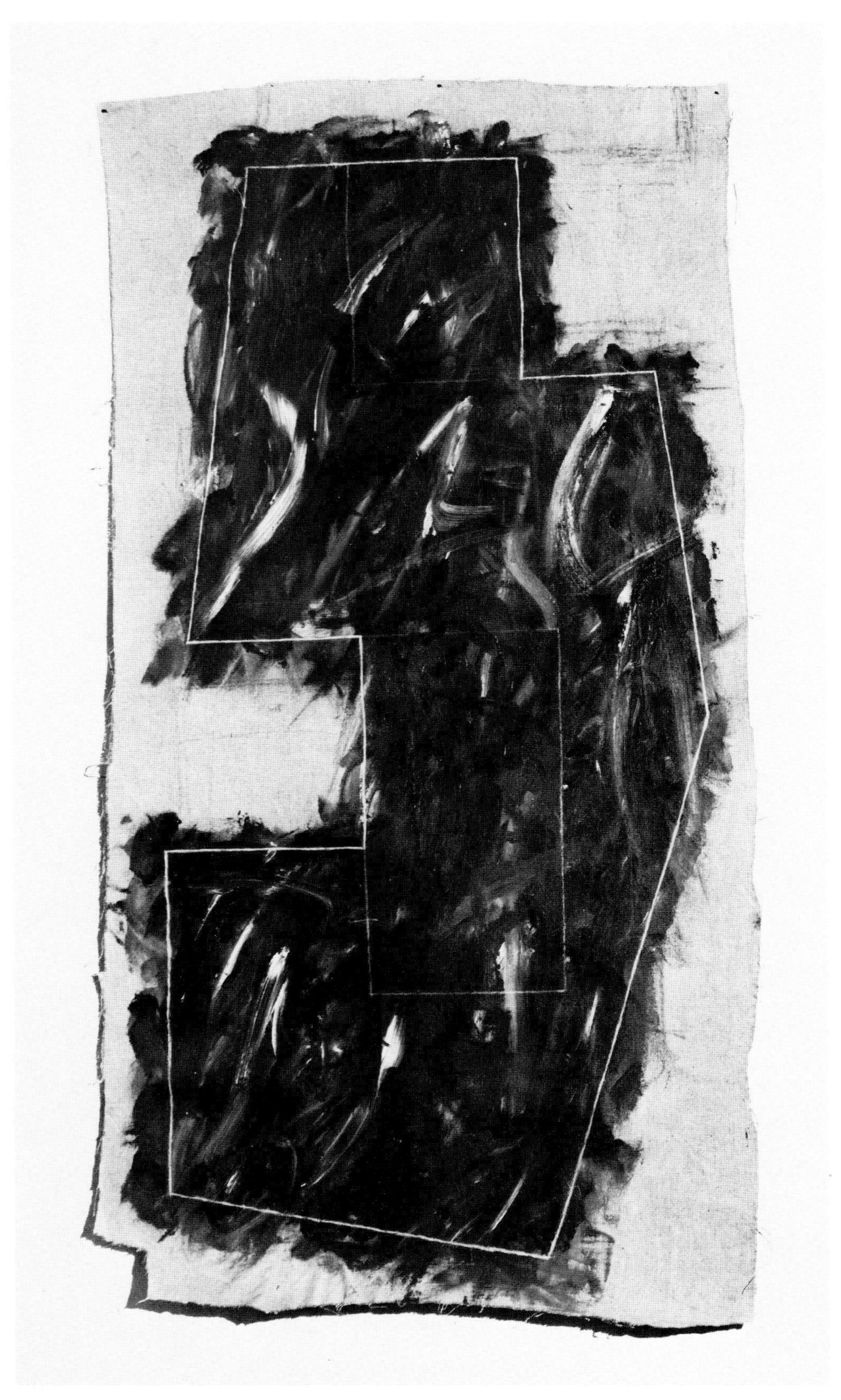

23. *Untitled*, 1982
acrylic and charcoal on linen
67 × 36½″

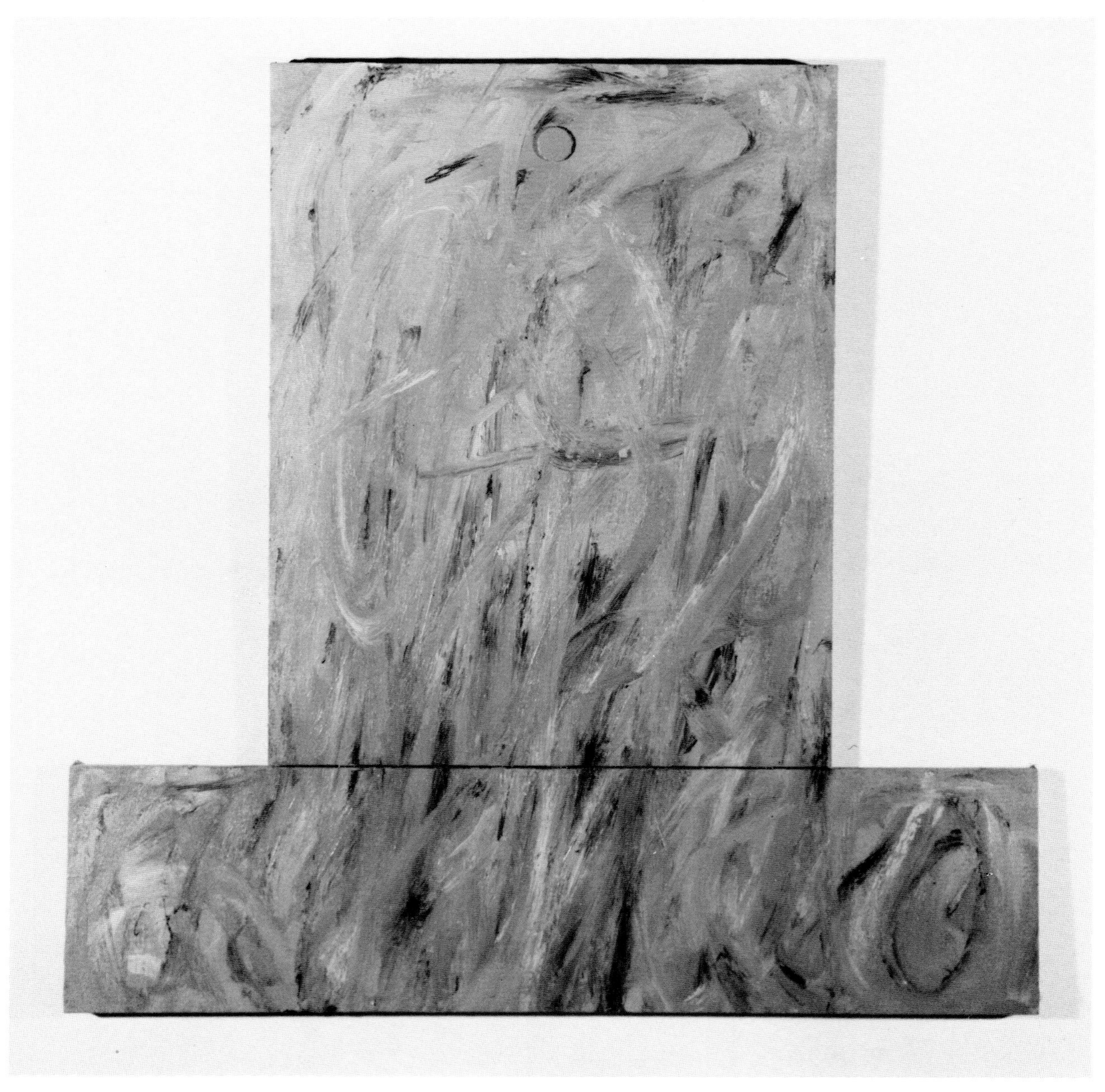

26. *Untitled*, 1982-83
    acrylic on canvas
    two parts:
    52 × 42″
    18 × 72″

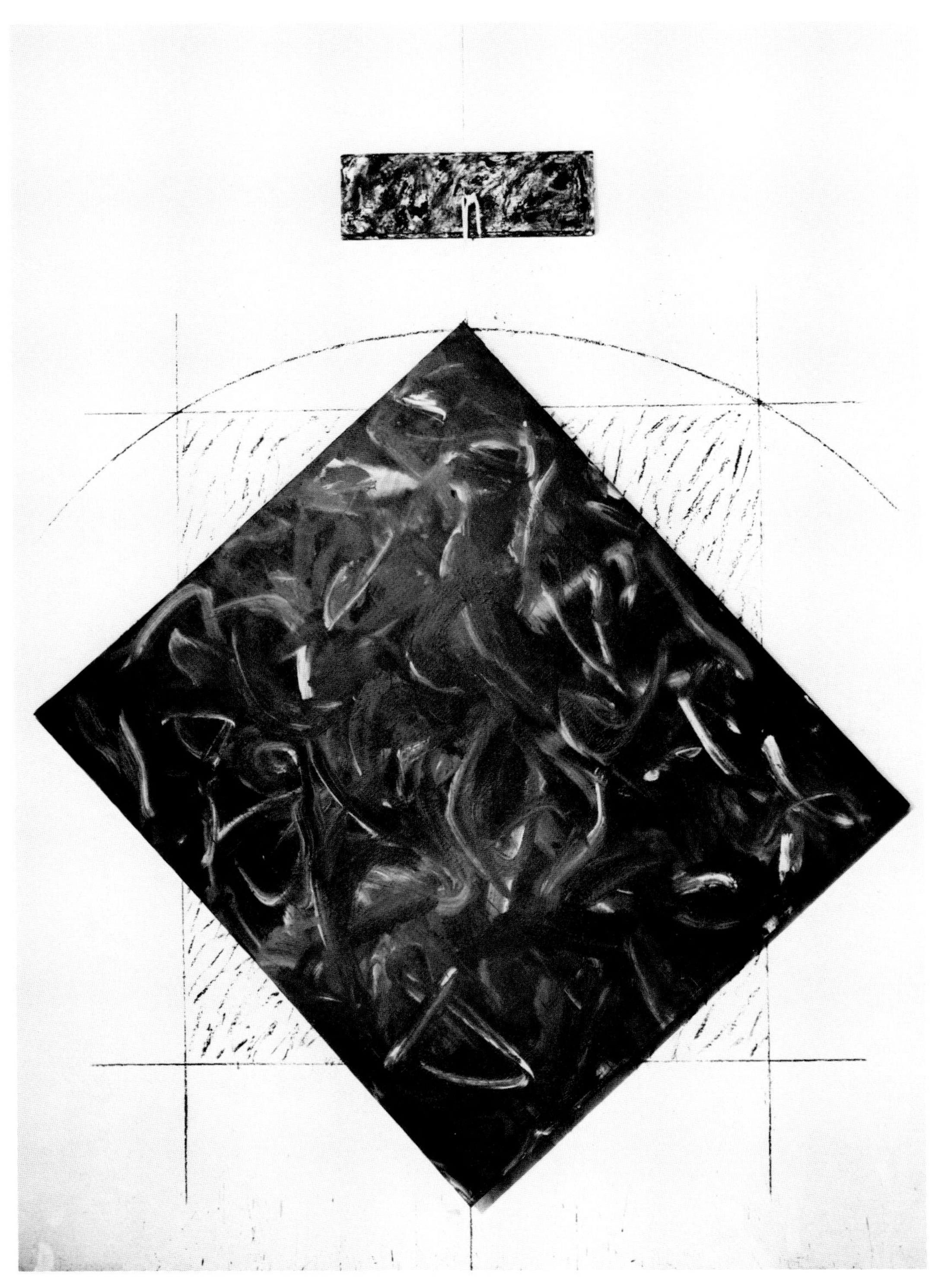

28. *Untitled*, 1982-83
    acrylic on canvas,
    acrylic on wood, charcoal on paper
    three parts:
    two, 51 × 57″ each
    7¾ × 22½″

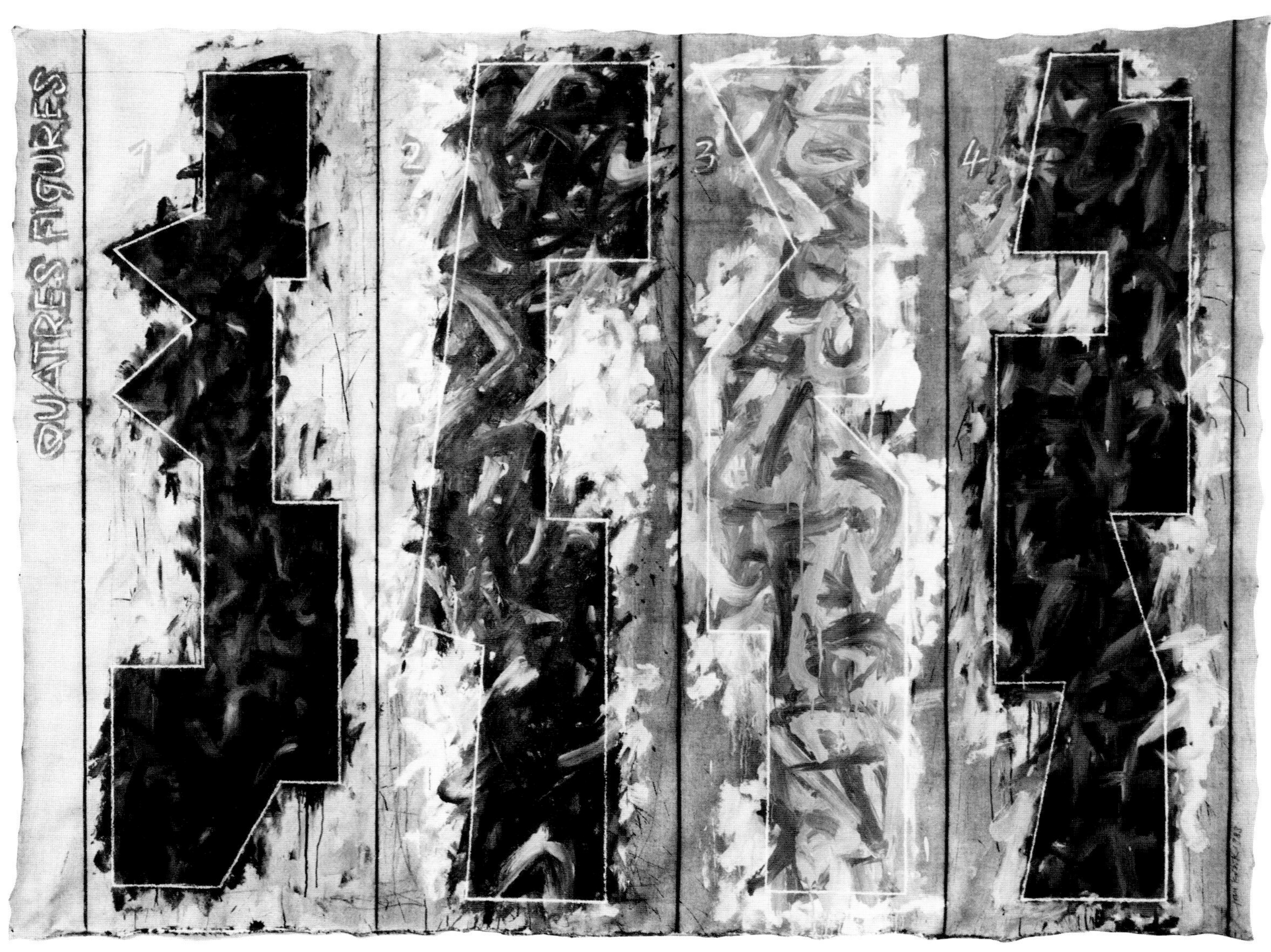

29. *Quatre Figures* [Four Figures], 1983
acrylic and charcoal on canvas
84¾ × 118⅛"

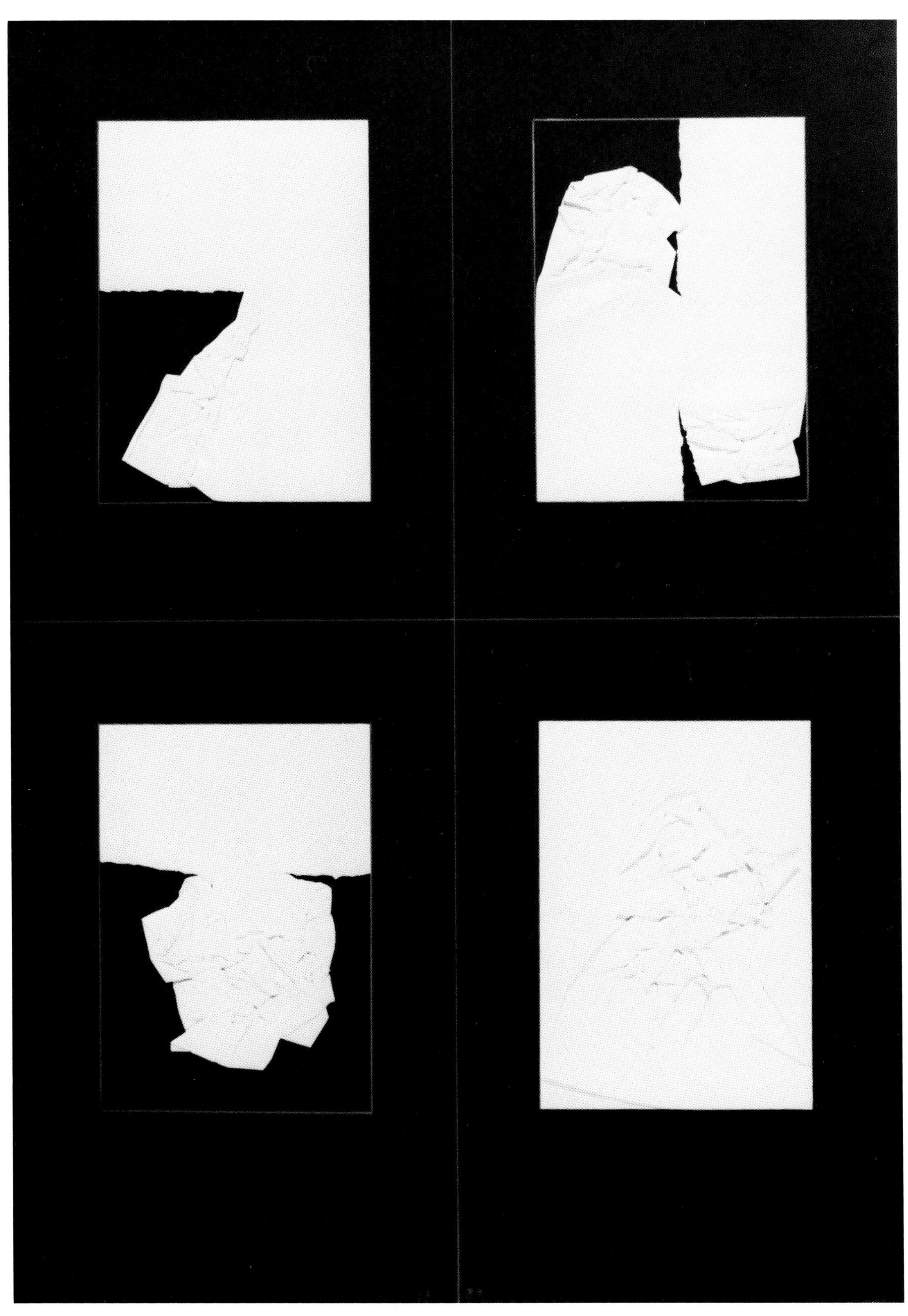

37. *Untitled,* 1980
    collage, graphite and ink on construction paper
    39 × 27½″

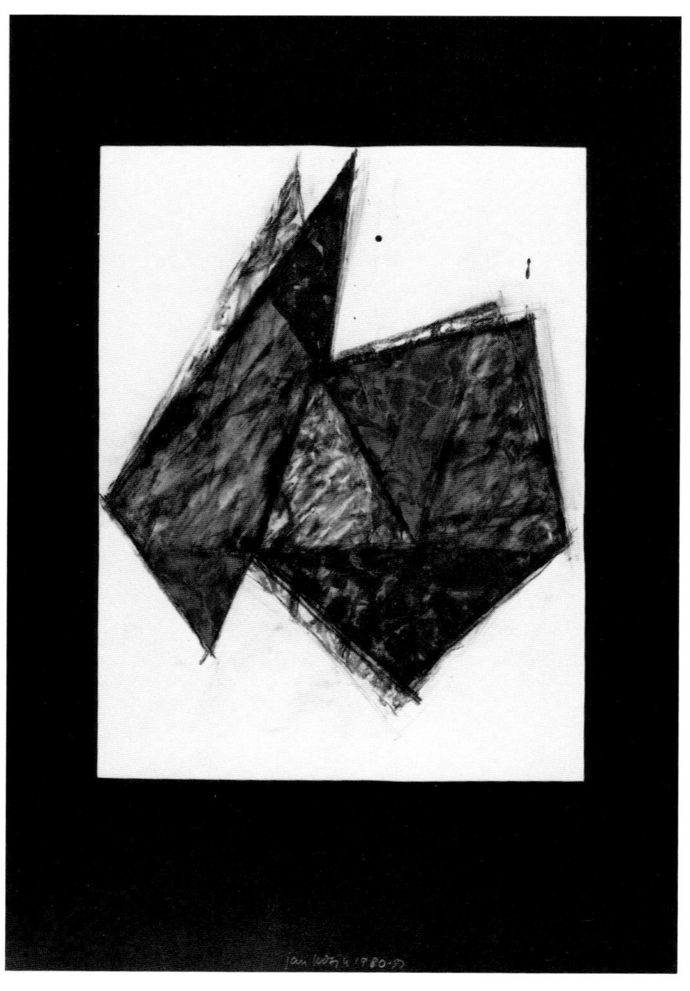

41. *Untitled,* 1980-81
    watercolor, acrylic and graphite on paper
    mounted on construction paper
    25½ × 19½″, mounted to 39 × 27½″

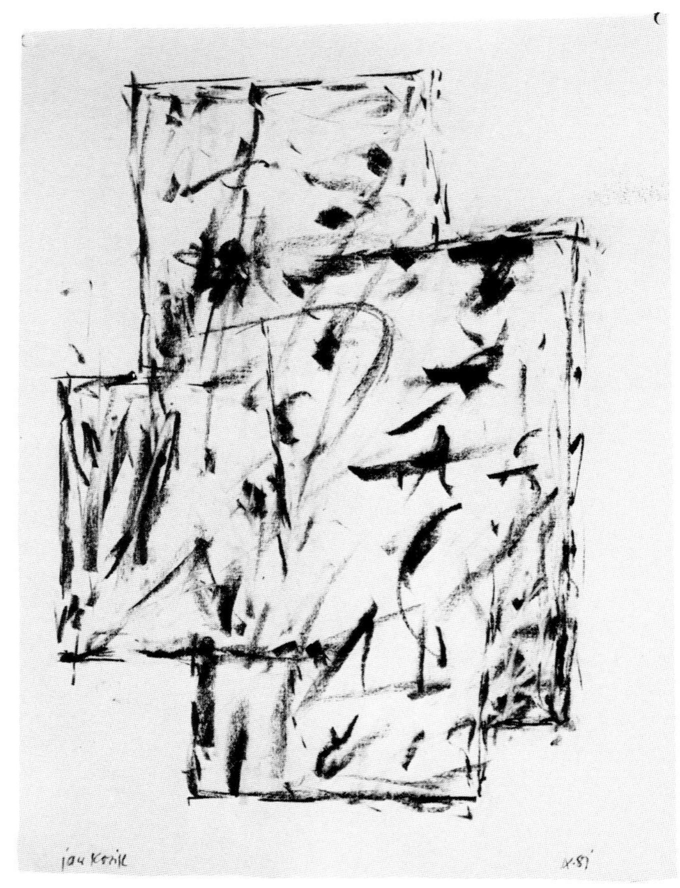

47. Untitled, 1981
    charcoal on paper mounted on board
    25½ × 18½″, mounted to 27½ × 19¾″

Catalogue of the Exhibition

Dimensions are given in inches, height preceding width
preceding depth. All works are collection of the artist
unless otherwise noted.

Asterisk (*) denotes work illustrated.

Paintings

*1. *Object transformable*
[Transformable object], 1972-73
acrylic on canvas, wood
dimensions variable
(fabric: 26 × 35″)

2. *Untitled*, 1973-74
acrylic on canvas
dimensions variable
(fabric: 53¼ × 82¾″)
Private Collection

*3. *Untitled*, 1975-76
acrylic on canvas, wood
56 × 13″

*4. *Untitled*, 1976-77
acrylic on canvas,
57½ × 52½″

5. *Untitled*, 1976-77
acrylic on canvas, string
66 × 39¼″

*6. *Untitled*, 1976-77
acrylic on canvas, string
27 × 37″

7. *Untitled*, 1977
acrylic on canvas, string
42½ × 84″

*8. *Untitled*, 1977
acrylic on canvas, string
48½ × 29⅛″

9. *Untitled*, 1978
acrylic on canvas, string
50 × 50″

10. *Untitled*, 1980
acrylic on canvas, string
52½ × 58¼″

*11. *Untitled* , 1980
tempera and wax on canvas
two parts:
78¾ × 78¾″
19½ × 19½″

*12. *Untitled*, 1980
acrylic on canvas, wood
two parts:
57 × 51″
2 × 79 × ½″

*13. *Untitled*, 1980
acrylic and aluminum on canvas, plastic
two parts:
31½ × 78¾″
27½ × 39⅜″

14. *Untitled*, 1980
tempera and wax on canvas, rope, wood
three parts:
28¾ × 52⅜″
67¾ × 78¾″
17 × 78¾″

*15. *Untitled*, 1980
wax, tempera and charcoal on canvas, acrylic,
graphite and aluminum on wood, chain
three parts:
29⅛ × 59⅛″
61⅛ × 59⅛″
2 × 78¾ × 1½″

16. *Untitled*, 1980
acrylic on canvas
three parts:
19½ × 44½″
39 × 29¼″
39 × 15″

17. *Untitled*, 1981
lacquer on wood
55¼ × 19½″

*18. *Untitled*, 1981
charcoal and stain on canvas
49 × 38¼″

*19. *Untitled*, 1981
acrylic and charcoal on canvas, wood
three parts:
19½ × 44½″
39 × 15″
39 × 29¼″

*20. *Untitled*, 1982
acrylic on canvas, wood
three parts:
42 × 52″
72 × 18″
4 × 73⅝ × 2″

*21. *Untitled*, 1982
acrylic on canvas, rope
two parts:
51 × 42″
72 × 18″

*22. *Untitled*, 1982
acrylic on paper board
30½ × 30″
Collection Steven and Cecile Biltekoff, Buffalo

*23. *Untitled*, 1982
acrylic and charcoal on linen
67 × 36½″

24. *Untitled*, 1982
acrylic on canvas
42 × 52″
Collection Monika Babackova, Brooklyn,
New York

*25. *Untitled*, 1982-83
acrylic on canvas
four parts:
two, 72 × 18″ each
42 × 52″
30 × 52″

*26. *Untitled*, 1982-83
acrylic on canvas
two parts:
52 × 42″
18 × 72″

*27. *Untitled*, 1982-83
acrylic on canvas
two parts:
18 × 72″
42 × 52″

*28. *Untitled*, 1982-83
acrylic on canvas,
acrylic on wood, charcoal on paper
three parts:
two, 51 × 57″ each
7¾ × 22½″

*29. *Quatre Figures* [Four Figures], 1983
acrylic and charcoal on canvas
84¾ × 118⅛″

30. *Untitled*, 1983
acrylic on canvas, wood
three parts:
two, 52 × 42″ each
52 × ½″

Works on Paper

31. *Untitled*, 1976
graphite and pastel on paper mounted on construction paper
25 × 17¼″, mounted to 39 × 27½″

32. *Untitled*, 1976
pastel on paper mounted on construction paper
39 × 27½″

33. *Untitled*, 1976
graphite and pastel on paper
21 × 15¾″

34. *Untitled*, 1976-77
graphite and aluminum on paper mounted on construction paper
30 × 19½″, mounted to 39 × 27½″

35. *Untitled*, 1979
charcoal on paper, construction paper collage
27½ × 21¾″

36. *Untitled*, 1980
watercolor, graphite and gouache on paper
mounted on construction paper
two drawings:
3⅜ × 3⅛″
13 × 15½″, mounted to 13¾ × 19½″

*37. *Untitled*, 1980
collage, graphite and ink on construction paper
39 × 27½″

38. *Untitled*, 1980
watercolor and pencil on paper mounted on paper
14 × 10½″, mounted to 15¾ × 12″

39. *Untitled*, 1980
watercolor and pencil on paper
mounted on construction paper
12¾ × 9¾″, mounted to 15¾ × 11¾″

40. *Untitled*, 1980
graphite, charcoal, pastel, watercolor and collage
mounted on construction paper
five drawings:
5½ × 20½″ each, mounted to 39 × 27½″

*41. *Untitled*, 1980-81
watercolor, acrylic and graphite on paper
mounted on construction paper
25½ × 19½″, mounted to 39 × 27½″

42. *Untitled*, 1981
watercolor, acrylic and pencil on paper
mounted on paper
13 × 9½″, mounted to 15¾ × 11¾″

43. *Untitled*, 1981
watercolor and graphite on Xerox
16½ × 11¾″

44. *Untitled*, 1981
pastel on Xerox
15¾ × 11¾″

45. *Untitled*, 1981
acrylic and ink on paper
25½ × 19½″

46. *Untitled*, 1981
pastel on Xerox
15¾ × 11¾″

*47. Untitled, 1981
charcoal on paper mounted on board
25½ × 18½″, mounted to 27½ × 19¾″

48. *Untitled*, 1982
acrylic on paper
61½ × 48″

Chronology

49. *Untitled,* 1982
acrylic and pastel on paper
61½ × 48″

50. *Untitled,* 1983
gesso and acrylic on paper
61½ × 48″

51. *Untitled,* 1982
charcoal on paper
61½ × 40½″

52. *Untitled,* 1982
acrylic and pastel on paper
61½ × 48″

53. *Untitled,* 1982
charcoal on paper
17¾ × 12¼″

54. *Untitled,* 1983
watercolor, graphite and aluminum on paper
12 × 17″

55. *Untitled,* 1983
acrylic, watercolor and pastel on paper
mounted on construction paper
30 × 22¼″, mounted to 39 × 27½″

1916
Born in Turnov, Czechoslovakia, son of Czech painter and teacher Pravoslav Kotik (1889-1970). Spends childhood in Turnov and (after family moves in 1924) in Mladá Boleslav among avant-garde artistic milieux. Begins painting at early age.

1932-34
Studies lithography and typography in Turnov. Moves to Prague in 1934.

1935-41
Studies at School for Applied Arts, Prague.

1936
First exhibition in vestibule of E.F. Burians Theater, Prague.

1937
Receives silver medal for contribution to Czechoslovakian Pavilion, World's Fair, Paris.

1939
Painting career is interrupted and imminent departure to Paris on government fellowship canceled after Hitler's military occupation of Czechoslovakia in March. Joins the Resistance, in which he participates for the duration of World War II.

1940
Marries Paula Epstein.

1941-43
Teaches at private art school.

1942
Founding member of *Gruppe 42,* an association of artists, poets and scholars committed to reflecting contemporary urban life in their work (disbands in 1948). Although they have no dogmatic program, many of the visual artists work in styles influenced by Cubism and Surrealism and paint themes of everyday life. Birth of son Petr.

1943
German occupational authorities forbid him to exhibit or teach through 1945. Birth of son Martin.

1945-46
With end of World War II, artists' activities and exhibitions increase. Visits France and Finland. Meets Alvar Aalto, which subsequently influences his thought.

1947
Works in various directorial posts of industrial design atelier, Ústředí lidové umělecké výroby (ULUV), Center for Applied Arts, Prague, until 1953, after which he remains a consultant.

1948
Government fellowship awarded for study in Paris is rescinded after the communist takeover.

1949-56
Forbidden to exhibit or sell paintings during Stalinist era, at which time Social Realism was only accepted style. Continues working in industrial design, glass making,

and book design (through 1969); paints in abstract style privately. Begins association with periodical *Tvar*, in which he publishes frequently through 1963.

1956
Meets Asger Jorn during organization of conference, "Mouvement international pour un Bauhaus imaginiste," (MIBI) in Alba, Italy. First contact with contemporary art and artists after isolation of previous years.

1957
Major one-artist exhibition at Galerie Československého Spisovatele (formerly Galerie Topič), Prague, the first showing of modern Czech art made during Stalinist era.

1958
Further easing of artistic constraints with Khrushchev reforms (1956-64). Makes large glasswork for Czechoslovakian Pavilion, World's Fair, Brussels, for which he wins second prize.

1961
Invited to participate in Carnegie International. Prohibited from exhibiting by Czech authorities.

1962
Extended stay in Moscow in conjunction with exhibition of Czechoslovakian glasswork.

1962-68
Continues to increase foreign contacts. Travels, lectures and writes frequently. Active in Czechoslovakian Institute of Design and many artists' organizations. President of Czechoslovakian Council of Industrial Design, an advisory board for industry. Exhibits frequently.

1966
Resides in Paris as guest of Cité internationale des Arts.

1967
Makes glass for Czechoslovakian Pavilion, World's Fair, Montreal. Divorced.

1968
In Yugoslavia at time of Soviet invasion of Czechoslovakia. Travels to Vienna, then Stockholm. Marries journalist Ruth Meyerovičová.

1969
Returns briefly to Prague, leaves for West Berlin.

1970
Invited by Deutscher Akademischer Austauschdienst (DAAD) to Berliner Künstlerprogramm, West Berlin. Settles in West Berlin.

1980-81
Resides in Paris as guest of Ministère de la Culture— Cité internationale des Arts, from fall 1980 through spring 1981.

1982-83
Resides in New York from fall 1982 through winter 1983.

1984
Lives and works in West Berlin.

Selected Exhibitions

Selected One-Artist Exhibitions

Complete annotated exhibitions history and bibliography may be found in the exhibition catalogue, *Jan Kotik: Arbeiten 1970-78*. Bochum, West Germany: Museum Bochum, 1978. Documentation of exhibitions, based on available resources, is as complete as possible.

1946
Galerie Alšova síň, Prague.

1957
Galerie Československého Spisovatele (formerly Galerie Topič), Prague. *Jan Kotik: 1948-1956*. Catalogue, text by Jaromír Pečírka.

1959
Galleria Notizie, Turin, Italy.

1960
Galerie Alšova síň, Prague.
Galerie Contemporaine, Brussels.

1963
Oblastní Galerie [Regional Gallery], Liberéc, Czechoslovakia.

1965
Oblastní Galerie [Regional Gallery], Jihlava, Czechoslovakia.

1966
Galerie bratří Čapkú, Prague. [February.] Catalogue, text by Ludmila Vachtová.
Galerie Orlando Cedrino, Munich, West Germany. *Jan Kotik*, May 10 - June 30. Catalogue, texts by Raoul-Jean Moulin, Ludmila Vachtová.

1968
Výstavní síň Mánes [Exhibition Hall], Prague. *Jan Kotik: 1939-1968*, [May-June]. Catalogue, text by Ludmila Vachtová.

1971
Haus am Lützowplatz, West Berlin. *Jan Kotik*, February 19 - March 28. Organized by Deutscher Akademischer Austauschdienst (DAAD). Catalogue, texts by R. Wedewer, Peter Nestler.

1972
Galerie Tanit, Munich, West Germany. *Jan Kotik: Objekte und Collagen*, December 8 - January 31, 1973. Catalogue, texts by Peter Nestler, Raoul-Jean Moulin.

1975
Amerika Haus, West Berlin. *Jan Kotik: Ritualisierung der Zeit*, [April - May]. Organized by Berliner Künstlerprogramm, Deutscher Akademischer Austauschdienst (DAAD). Brochure, text by Arsén Pohribný, artist's statement.

1978
Museum Bochum, Bochum, West Germany. *Jan Kotik: Arbeiten, 1970-78*, October 21 - November 26. Catalogue, text by Arsén Pohribný, chronology by Peter Spielmann, artist's statement. Traveled (with additional works and addendum to above catalogue) to Orangerie,

Schloss Charlottenburg, West Berlin as *Jan Kotik, Arbeiten 1970-79*, November 15 - December 16, 1979, under the auspices of Neuer Berliner Kunstverein in conjunction with Senator für Kulturelle Angelegenheiten.

1981
Petersen Galerie, West Berlin. *Jan Kotik: Komprimationen & recelagen + 2 wandobjekte*, January 9 - February 20. Brochure, artist's statement.

1982
Geneviève et Serge Mathieu [Gallery], Besançon, France. *Kotik: sculptures, peintures*, [March]. Brochure.

1983
Bethune Gallery, State University of New York at Buffalo, Buffalo. *Jan Kotik: Works on Paper*, January 27 - February 14.
Galerie Marina Dinkler and Galerie Petersen (concurrently), West Berlin. *Jan Kotik: Wandobjekte und Zeichnungen*, March 15 - April 30. Brochure, interview with the artist by Marina Dinkler and Jes Petersen.

Selected Group Exhibitions

1941
Galerie Topič (later Galerie Československého Spisovatele), Prague. *Konfrontation I*, [fall].

1942
Galerie Jungmannovo Náměstí, Prague. *Konfrontation II*, [spring].

1943
Galerie Topič (later Galerie Československého Spisovatele), Prague. *Gruppe 42* exhibition. Also in *Gruppe 42* exhibitions in Czechoslovakia at regional galleries in Nová Paka (1942); Prague (1945); Brno (1946, catalogue essay by Jindřich Chalupecký); Ostrava, [n.d.]; Bratislava (1946).

1956
[Alternative space], Alba, Italy. Exhibition in conjunction with "Congrès du Mouvement international pour un Bauhaus imaginiste" (MIBI).

1959
Palazzo Graneri, Turin, Italy. *Arte nuova: esposizione internazionale di pittura e scultura*, May 5 - June 15. Organized by Circolo degli Artisti. Catalogue, introduction by Luciano Pistoi, essay by Michel Tapié.

1962
Chateau Rychnov, Rychnov, Czechoslovakia. Festival of Contemporary Art. Also in 1963.

1964
XXXII Biennale di Venezia, Venice, Italy. Czechoslovakian Pavilion, June 20 - October 18. Catalogue, text by Miroslav Mičko, pp. 198-200.

1965
Haus am Lützowplatz, West Berlin. *Kotik/Kolař/Koblasa*.

Städtische Kunstgalerie, Bochum, West Germany. *Profile V: Tschechoslowakische Kunst Heute*, May 16 - July 25. Catalogue, texts by Jiří Kotalík, Miroslav Mičko. Traveled to Staatliche Kunsthalle, Baden-Baden, West Germany. October 8 - November 4.

1966
Akademie der Künste, West Berlin. *Tschechoslowakische Kunst der Gegenwart*, July 17 - August 21. Catalogue, introduction by Hans Scharoun, text by Jindřich Chalupecký.

Galerie Václava Špály, Prague. *Obraz a písmo* [Picture and Script], January 14 - February 6. Catalogue, texts by Jiří Padrta, Zdeněk Felix. Traveled to Oblastní Galerie [Regional Gallery], Jihlava, Czechoslovakia; Muzeum Kolín, Kolín, Czechoslovakia.

1968
Slovenská Národná Galéria, Bratislava, Czechoslovakia. *50let Československého Malířství, 1918-1968* [50 Years of Czechoslovakian Painting], May - June. Organized in conjunction with Narodní Galeríe, Prague. Catalogue, texts by Jiří Kotalík, Karol Vaculìk. Traveled to Alšova Jihočeská Galerie, Hluboká nad Vltavou, Czechoslovakia; Moravská Galerie, Brno, Czechoslovakia; Galerie Výtvarného Umèní, Ostrava, Czechoslovakia.

Výstavní síň Mánes [Exhibition Hall], Prague. *Nová citlivost* [New Sensibilities], July 19 - August 18. Catalogue, text by Jiří Padrta.

1970
Rath Museum, Geneva, Switzerland. *Art tchèque du XXe siècle*, May 26 - June 28. Catalogue, text by Jiří Kotalík. Traveled to Kunsthaus, Zürich, Switzerland as *Tschechische Kunst des 20 Jahrhunderts: Einige Aspekte der Entwicklung*. Catalogue, introduction by Felix Baumann, text by Jiří Kotalík.

1971
Kunsthalle Nürnberg, Nuremberg, West Germany. *II Biennale Nürnberg: Künstler-Theorie-Work*, April 30 - August 1. Catalogue.

1973
Beethoven-Halle, Bonn. *30 internationale Künstler in Berlin*, December 14-27. Organized by Deutscher Akademischer Austauschdienst (DAAD). Catalogue, texts by Karl Ruhrberg, Roland Wiegenstein, Jürgen Harten.

1974
Musée d'art moderne de la ville de Paris, Paris. *Salon de Mai*, [May]. Also in 1975.

1975
Messe-Gelände, West Berlin. *Freie Berliner Kunstausstellung: Section Gruppe Systhema*. Also in 1976.

Dortmund, West Germany. *23 Jahresausstellung des Deutschen Künstlerbundes: Geschichte und Gegenwart*, April 11 - May 25. Catalogue.

1976
XXXVII Biennale di Venezia, Venice, Italy. *Attualità internazionali 1972-76*. Catalogue.

Multihalle, Herzogenriedpark, Mannheim, West Germany. *24 Jahresausstellung des Deutschen Künstlerbundes*, May 31 - July 18. Catalogue.

1977
Amos Anderson Museum, Helsinki. [Exhibition of *Gruppe Systhema*.]

Galerie Bossin, West Berlin. [Exhibition of *Gruppe Systhema*.]

1978
Akademie der Künste, Neue Nationalgalerie and Staatliche Kunsthalle, West Berlin. *26 Jahresausstellung des Deutschen Künstlerbundes*, November 20 - January 3, 1979. Catalogue.

[Alternative space, Lützowstrasse], West Berlin. *Räume*. Also in 1979 exhibition, *Situationen*.

Galerie Krüll, Krefeld, West Germany [Exhibition of *Gruppe Systhema*.] Catalogue, texts by Karl Ruhrberg, Richard Paul Lohse.

Galerie Loeb, Bern. [Exhibition of *Gruppe Systhema*.]

1979
Kunstgebäude, Stuttgart, West Germany. *27 Jahresausstellung des Deutschen Künstlerbundes*, September 29- November 4. Catalogue.

1980
Kunstverein, Hanover, West Germany. *28 Jahresausstellungen des Deutschen Künstlerbundes: Kunst auf Papier, Kunst mit Papier* and *Material elementale*, September 27 - November 9. Catalogue.

Büro Berlin, West Berlin.

1981
Kunsthalle Nürnberg, Germanisches Nationalmuseum, and Norishalle, Nuremberg, West Germany. *29 Jahresausstellung des Deutschen Künstlerbundes*, September 26 - November 8. Catalogue.

1982
[Alternative space, AEG-Fabrik, Ackerstrasse], West Berlin. *Künstquartier: Ausländische Künstler in Berlin*, May 14 - June 17. Organized by Interessengemeinschaft Berliner Kunsthändler. Catalogue, introduction by Michael Nungesser.

Kunstpalast, Dusseldorf, West Germany. *30 Jahresausstellung des Deutschen Künstlerbundes — Thema: Sequenzen - Varianten*, August 29 - October 3. Catalogue.

1983
Gropius-Bau, West Berlin. *30 Jahresausstellung des Deutschen Künstlerbundes*, November 3 - January 4, 1984. Catalogue.

Untitled study for *Wall-construction,* 1979, pencil and pen on Xerox, 11⅝ x 8¼″. Collection of the artist.

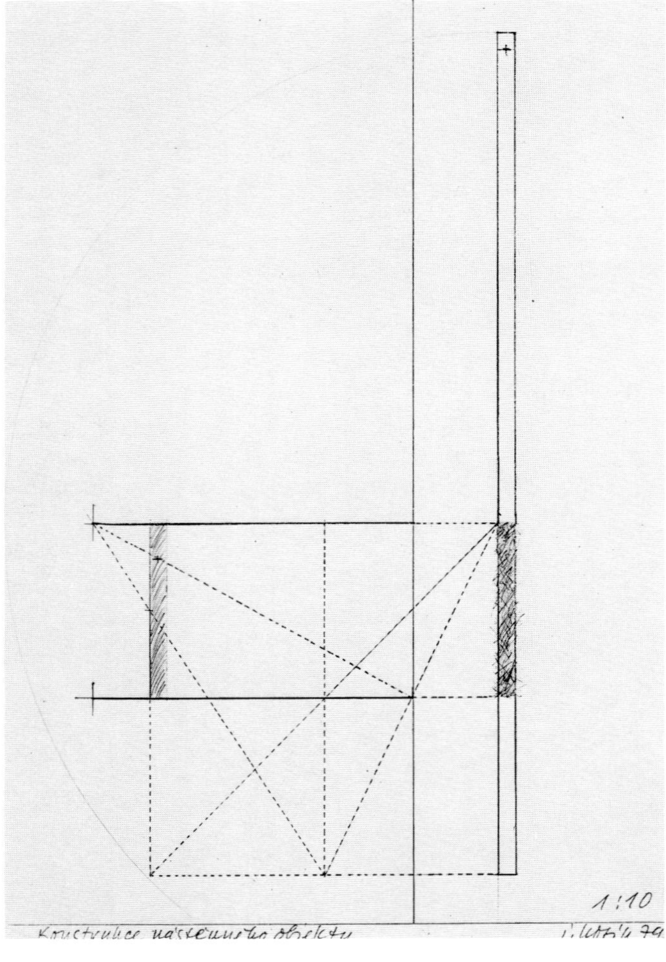

Selected Bibliography

By the Artist

1954
Pardice a kultura československé vyrobý. Prague: Verlag
Orbis. [Compiled writings.]

1959
[*Et al.*] "Spolupráce architektury, vytvarného a užitého
umění." *Výtvarné Umění* (Prague), no. 9, pp. 54-63.
[Contributions by K. Honzík, J Kotik, V. Sychra, and M.
Lamač on the limits and possibilities of collaboration be-
tween architects and visual artists.]

1963
[Article on El Greco.] *Výtvarná Práce* (Prague), vol. 11,
no. 25-26, p. 7.
Ponámky o srozumitelnosti uměleckeho díla. *Výtvarná
Práce (Prague)*, vol. 11, no. 13-14, pp. 4-5.

1964
"Rembrandtova *Danae.*" *Výtvarná Práce* (Prague), vol.
12, no. 23, p. 7.

1967
[Article on color in the work of Bohumíl Kubista.] *Výtvarná Práce* (Prague), vol. 15, no. 19, pp. 1, 7, 11.

1969
O užitećnosti věcí. Prague: Obelisk. [Compiled writings.]

1971
"System INOMAGO." *Mitteilungen des Instituts für
moderne Kunst* (Nuremberg), no. 2-3, n.p.

1974
Konsum oder Verbrauch. Hamburg: Hoffman und
Campe. [Compiled writings.]

On the Artist

1960
Ashton, Dore. "News from behind the iron curtain."
ARTnews (New York), vol. 59, no. 7, November, pp. 31,
58-60.

Vachtová, Ludmila. "Cinque pittori cecoslovacchi." *La
Biennale di Venezia* (Venice), vol. 10, no. 39,
pp. 24-34.

1961
Restany, Pierre. "Prague." *Das Kunstwerk* (Stuttgart),
no. 14, February, pp. 23-25.

1963
Vachtová, Ludmila. "Jan Kotik in Libérec." *Výtvarná
Práce* (Prague), vol. 11, no. 11-12, n.p.

1965
Felix, Zdeněk. "Maliřovo Ohlednuti." *Výtvaná Práce*
(Prague), vol. 13, no. 27, pp. 6, 8.

1966
Padrta, Jiři. "Nová Formálnost a Obsahovost v Obrazech
Jana Kotíka." *Výtvarná Práce* (Prague), vol. 14,
no. 5, pp. 4-5.

1967
Restany, Pierre. "Prague: Sisyphe sans Kafka serait
Prométhée." *Domus* (Milan), no. 450, May, pp. 50-54.

1968
Kotalík, Jiří. *Kunst unserer Zeit.* Cologne: DuMont
Schauberg Verlag.

Vachtová, Ludmila. "Okölo Jana Kotíka." *Výtvarné
Umění* (Prague), vol. VIII, no. 18, n.p.

1970
Dusăn, Šindelář. *Socasne umelecke sklo v ceskosloven-
sku.* Prague: Obelisk.

1971
Moulin, Raoul-Jean. "Jan Kotik: Lecture et Manipula-
tion." *Les Lettres Françaises* (Paris), no. 1455, October
11, p. 28.

1977
Pohribný, Arsén. Untitled text: *Schwarz auf Weiss, Dok-
umentation über visuelle Operationen* (Dusseldorf), no.
4, November, p. 2, [Special issue on Jan Kotik].

Public Collections

Arthotek, West Berlin.

Collection of the Federal Republic of Germany, Bonn.

Konstrådet [Arts Council], Stockholm.

Moravská Galerie [Moravian Gallery], Brno,
Czechoslovakia.

Museum Bochum, Bochum, West Germany.

Museum hlavního mèsta Prahy [Gallery of the City of
Prague], Prague.

Muzej na sovremenata umetnost [Museum of Contemporary Art], Skopje, Yugoslavia.

Narodní Galerie [National Gallery], Prague.

Nationalgalerie, West Berlin.

Oblastní Galerie [Regional Gallery], Ostrava,
Czechoslovakia.

Oblastní Galerie [Regional Gallery], Pardubice,
Czechoslovakia.

Oblastní Galerie [Regional Gallery], Roudnice,
Czechoslovakia.

Severočeska Galerie [North Bohemian Gallery], Liberec,
Czechoslovakia.

Středočeská Galerie [Central Bohemian Gallery],
Roudnice, Czechoslovakia.

Photographic Credits

Werner Bethsold: p. 2
Courtesy of the artist: pp. 8, 9 (left and right), 11 (top
and bottom), 13, 14, 17, 18, 22, 28, 29 (bottom), 31, 32,
33, 35, 36, 38, 41, 44 (bottom).
Biff Henrich: pp. 34, 40, 43, 44 (top).
Zybnek Sedo: p. 25 (top, middle, and bottom).
Werner Vogel: pp. 27, 29 (top), 30, 37, 38, 39, 42.